ON GOVERNANCE

Cor Publicum:
The Evolution of Res Publica

FRANCA BARONI

Samsara
Press

ON GOVERNANCE
Cor Publicum: The Evolution of Res Publica
By Franca Baroni

Cover and text design by Carol Hiltner
Proofreading by Laurie Masters
Cover photo by © iStockphoto.com/joecicak
Publishing Logo by John Palombo
Printed by AlphaGraphics

Published by Samsara Press, Seattle, WA
www.corpublicum.us
You can contact the author at her website:
www.corpublicum.com

ISBN: 978-0-9833415-6-7

First Special Edition February 11, 2011
Printed in the United States.

To Loyce
with deep
gratitude & love,
thank you for
who you are!

6/25/12

*An invitation from an individual Heart
to the collective Heart.*

*Heart Wisdom continues to fearlessly explore,
while the mind claims, compartmentalizes,
disbelieves, dissects, dismisses,
fears, and even rages.*

(Cor: the Latin word for heart)

Contents

Introduction

The old structures of power and control are no longer adequate to hold the new incoming vibration of consciousness as the old collective contract is disintegrating. The need to hold on to the old failing structure increases as the systems of society are collapsing. Many new systems are emerging and many are disintegrating rapidly, because they are formed on the old rigid vertical structure of power and control. In this general hysteria of a collapsing world, governments and organizations have struggled to maintain control. Some practices are well meant; others are manipulative and meant to maintain a sense of stability to appease an erupting collective.

As this long-standing social contract is coming to a natural end, the fear of being unable to handle the freedom that brought forth the old social contract in the first place is re-emerging: the responses to this fear are many: calling out for more regulations to re-enact another version of the social contract based on the old power and control structure; rebelling against the establishment out of an *us versus them* mind-set, rooted in yet the same belief of control and power.

The key to the re-emergence of governance is surrendering to the death of this old social contract. This act takes tremendous courage. It is the courage to dwell in the transition, in the space between death and life, in the realm of formlessness where as a nation we lose our sense of identity—where we are to let go of what defines us as an organized collective, a state, a nation, an international entity.

As a collective, we never really made the leap into freedom. We have been in the grip of hierarchical forms of government for thousands of years, because of our deep-rooted fear of being unable to handle the unknown—formlessness—and because we have been equating freedom with brutality and the rule of the fittest. For the same reason we have destroyed other healthier forms of government. It is time for making this leap, and if we have the courage to dwell in the unknown of what is next, the new form will emerge more readily and it will most likely be a healthier form, rather than a twisted version of the old form.

Letting go of what defines us allows us to reconnect to what we truly value in a deeper way. It is in the questioning of old assumptions about how we are governing ourselves that we can start to strengthen the foundation of governance. It is in the spaciousness of a pause that new creative thinking can emerge. If we keep scrambling, trying to rescue the old forms, refusing to question the old assumptions that our social contract and forms of government rest upon, our collective will be a sinking ship with no reason to re-emerge. However, if we surrender to the fact that we are sinking and trust in the wisdom of the sinking, we will emerge from the deep water with a new ship headed to shore, carrying the evolving organic body of a new system of governance.

Part I

Old Social Contract: The Grid

Chapter 1

Grid

The Grid is the vibrational social contract or software on which the collective consciousness is founded. The collective consciousness feeds this social contract by each choice and action, and the social contract in turn is fed intermittently by the choices of the collective. A continuous exchange of basic vibrational values, programs, and agreements determines the functioning and values of our society at large. Each individual, family, organization, state, nation, and ethnic group has its own peculiar social contract, but each is ultimately linked to the Grid. The degree to which each entity is linked to the Grid depends on the consciousness that it holds.

The Grid is the core agreement on which our political, legal, economic, health, and other systems are based. The shapes and forms of these systems vary. And their philosophical roots, which justify their existence no matter how elaborate, are still grounded in the basic human operating system: the Grid.

The Grid rests upon basic vibrational values. *Per se* it is always changing, but if it is fed the same information continuously through experience, it is strengthened in its core vibration. Some of the core vibrational beliefs and values are that as human beings, thus as citizens, we are not capable of managing freedom in a responsible way; that we are untrustworthy; that we are not lovable; that we are alone against the world; that the world is a dangerous place; that money and status are the sources of power and control; that we are incapable of dealing with complexity; and that we are unworthy and incapable of holding power.

The beliefs and values contained in the Grid are obviously validated in our *known* history, as well as daily, by experiences that lead us to delegate power to an external entity that can at best cope with the dysfunction. Because the concept of power originates from the Grid, this power can generate only "solutions" that match the vibration of the Grid. And, the ones to whom the power has been delegated—governments and organizations—are consequently a vibrational match to the beliefs and values contained in the Grid: untrustworthy, heartless, corrupt, greedy, and at times even dangerous. This is what self-sabotage and enslavement means.

Chapter 2

Lost Freedom

Freedom is a desperate cry for oxygen in a world that is suffocating from its own destructive consciousness and enslavement. The cry for freedom is one of an adult who believes himself to be a child and from his crib cries for permission to jump over the bars, all the while having long mastered the ability to leap.

> *Freedom in the consciousness of enslavement remains but a mirage and an endless quest, no matter the social, economic, or legal circumstances.*

Freedom in the consciousness of enslavement remains but a mirage and an endless quest, no matter the social, economic, or legal circumstances of the individual or collective asking for freedom. Freedom in the consciousness of Oneness is the untouchable essence inherent in each entity. The awareness of this essence is what unleashes the power to co-create reality, to govern ourselves in a life- affirming way. The awareness of this co-creative power and its intimate relationship with freedom is what perpetuates freedom. As soon as power is abused, i.e., out of sync with the wisdom of the Heart, with the vibration of Love, this power is doomed to shrink, and freedom is lost.

The quest for freedom is a cosmic joke, a starving human sitting on a bounty of delicious food, complaining about the lack of resources.

Chapter 3

De-Form of Governance and "Cropped" Law: Mind as Lone Monarch

Governance and Law are intimately connected. Ultimately is not everything Law? In our plane of existence we have created a separation, a cropping of Law. We have enclosed Law; we have forced Law into a rigid structure to control and determine the lives of people, thus creating law (lowercase). The philosophy underlying law as conceived in the annals and scriptures has been based on the premise of duality, a hierarchical structure of beliefs— a pyramidal structure.

> *We have enclosed Law; we have forced Law into a rigid structure to control and determine the lives of people, thus creating law.*

When law is conceived at its foundation as a rigid structure of rules, regulations, and policies, it is disconnected from the Laws governing reality and incapable of bringing justice and peace on the individual plane and at the macroscopic level. It is a law that always falls short, because it is anchored in the mental realm of consciousness.

All teachings of the great thinkers and philosophers who have found their way into the halls of power have been received, distilled, and articulated through the filters of the mind—the rational mind. That, *per se,* is a cropping of the message contained in these teachings, because teachings have to be filtered through the Heart to reach into the Hearts of people. These teachings have to pulsate with the core vibration of the Earth, with the core vibration of the universe, which is Love. This vibration has been cropped and segregated from the teachings and theories that currently determine the foundations of our very forms of government, constitutions, the rule of law, and other principles that govern the way we organize as a collective.

> *Love has been cropped and segregated from the teachings and theories that currently determine the foundations of our very forms of government.*

It is time now to listen to the new vibrations of Love, the new vibrations of the universal pulsations of justice, freedom, and equality that are seeking to enter into the halls of power and into the Hearts of people.

There is a lot of resistance and fear to letting the teachings of the Heart enter the realm of governance, because the Grid that currently controls the way the collective governs itself is locked into a dense fear vibration. The level of mistrust of Heart-based teachings as a new foundation of Law and governance is peaking, because the frequencies of Heart Wisdom are increasing. In this tension, the refusal to open the gates of consciousness is increased by a core mistrust held in the cellular matrix of each person. The lineage of mistrust vibrates at the cellular level, dating back thousands of years.

Unlocking the gate—and as we later discuss, unlocking the Grid—is the way the Love vibration enters Law and the foundations of governance.

The Love vibration cannot be captured and processed through the mind, which has been made the lone ruler and monarch of our plane of consciousness. True democracy remains a dream when it originates from the cropped space of the mind. True democracy emerges only from the formless space of Love. This space is unknown to the mind, because it cannot be articulated; it cannot be categorized; it cannot be compartmentalized. To the collective psyche this space is uncontrollable, dangerous, untrustworthy, and unreliable. It can be managed and acknowledged only in the exchange between individuals and in the realm of what we call religion or in modern-day terms spirituality.

This deep mistrust in the teachings of the Heart as a way to organize our co-existence is rooted in the core mistrust of our human experience, in the core fear and experience of being separate, of being sinful, of being incapable of embracing freedom. All these vibrations are contained in the Grid: at the cellular level and at the macroscopic level. Letting the teachings of the Heart "rule" and enter the

True democracy emerges only from the formless space of Love.

very definition of Law and the realm of governance is, to different degrees, a threatening proposition to each human being and to "the establishment."

New governance can emerge only when a new collective contract is embraced, when the collective connects to the web of Oneness consciousness. The vibrations of this web allow for the teachings of the Heart to enter our plane of existence, our cellular matrix, and thus allow for the foundations of governance and Law to change. A conscious collective choice opens the portal to a new way of living and experiencing "reality." This choice is the end of enslavement of the human species by the lone mind disconnected from the pulsation of life that originates from the Heart.

True democracy can emerge only when the teachings of the brilliant philosophers who have influenced our co-existence are freed from the exclusionary vibration of the mental plane, when they are grounded into the wisdom of the Heart. These teachings, however well articulated, remain locked in time and out of touch with the ever-evolving consciousness when the mind filters and interprets them. These teachings find their true completion if they are freed and allowed to flow and merge into the pool of Love, the vibration of compassion. At that point, they can become fully alive and capable of synchronizing with the universal Laws that govern reality, with the Hearts of the people, and with the complexities intrinsic to reality. Embracing the formlessness of Love as a foundation of governance and Law is an act of trust in our true essence as co-creative beings. It is an act of trust in our ability to create a benign world woven together by understanding, compassion, and cooperation.

> *Embracing the formlessness of Love as a foundation of governance and Law is an act of trust in our true essence as co-creative beings.*

In the last several centuries, we have agreed on and created a world ruled for the most part by a linear vertical hierarchical structure that is, *per se,* out of sync with nature, with the essence of how whole, sustainable forms are created. We have been living in a world that is out of sync with the fundamental Laws that rule existence. Our world is in continuous resistance to and at unending war with the wisdom of formlessness from which whole forms, whole Laws, whole systems of governance can emerge.

Law is currently operating at about 40% of its potential, because it is cropped from its foundation, which is the vibration of the Heart. When the gate to the Heart is opened, Law can be freed to find its wholeness, to reverberate into our Hearts, and to connect to the vibration of justice. As long as the vibration of justice is sought from mental linear constructs that are deeply entrenched in our current systems, justice remains a long-sought dream and ideal and can never be fully grounded in the Hearts and experiences of those whom it serves.

> *Law is currently operating at about 40% of its potential, because it is cropped from its foundation, which is the vibration of the Heart.*

If we were to use an anatomical analogy, our current body of law draws its life force exclusively from the brain. In flesh, such a body would be greatly hindered and would not survive long. A healthy human body draws its life force from a complex interplay of synchronized systems and organs that work to maximize life in the body. It is moved and sustained by this complex interplay, which is for the most part mysterious and unknown to the mind, and yet accepted. And most important, a body becomes dysfunctional and gradually dissolves if not nurtured by touch and Love.

Our collective consciousness has created a body of law and governance that originates from a mind that not only draws its life force exclusively from the brain but also denies that any other systems of the body are needed to function. Of course such a body is in constant survival mode, gasping for air; its life force is continuously draining.

The time has come to free Law and governance from the cage of the mind and let them be organized by the waves of consciousness and the wisdom of the Heart.

Chapter 4

Current Collective Agreements

Invariability and Separation

Collective agreements are variable in their nature. However, for the longest time the intrinsic and unconscious premise has been that these agreements are invariable. Invariability is an essential provision of the current social contract, and yet the essence of every agreement is that it is alterable, as alteration is the only way that the potential of creation is expressed. Creation happens through an act of choice and intention activating the vibrational possibility that translates into form.

The premise that fundamental agreements are frozen in time, unchangeable and irrefutable, is intrinsically disconnected from the essence of life, from the universal Laws that govern manifestation. Consciousness vibrates and is ever evolving, ever searching for new forms of expression and manifestation. In this sense, any agreement, if it is to be considered alive and capable of contributing to new life-affirming forms, must be flexible enough to accommodate the ever-changing spiral of reality. Life is a dance, a dance of expression, and any agreement that is limited in its expression is eventually meant to dissolve and disintegrate into form-lessness, which is the new starting point of creation.

When mental constructs lock it into a rigid structure, an agreement is out of sync with the natural cycle of consciousness and creation, and it inevitably creates unnatural and unsustainable effects. This is typical of the agreements contained in the Grid.

When mental constructs lock an agreement into a rigid structure, it is out of sync with the natural cycle of consciousness and creation, and it inevitably creates unnatural and unsustainable effects.

Again, the main agreement in the Grid is the one of immutability. Contained within this agreement is an assumption that immutability is the only way the collective is capable of managing the unmanageable, i.e., freedom. This agreement originates in the core belief that humanity and divinity are separate. It stems from the belief in the innate inability of humans to co-create in sync with Oneness consciousness. It is based on the ex-ternalization of the co-creative powers that have been placed exclusively in the hands of an external construct of governance or in the hands of a perceived God: a mental and ungrounded construct of authority and di-vinity untouchable by and separate from humans.

Divide and Conquer

The agreement described above is an expression of another core agreement of the Grid: *divide et impera* (divide and conquer), which permeates all agreements. As long as the *divide et impera* agreement is in place, connecting to Oneness consciousness is very difficult. This agreement is a thick filter through which the life force of Oneness consciousness can only trickle in at best. The *divide et impera* agreement, along with the immutability agreement, is the steel foundation of the Grid. Rigid and self-contained in its own downspiraling universe, this agreement is meant to disintegrate into formlessness—not because of a moral judgment (a lens through which systems and creations are often assessed) but simply because it cannot sustain life.

> *The* divide et impera *agreement rests on the fear of the wave of change.*

The *divide et impera* agreement, signed by the collective and included in its social contract—the Grid—is the main reason that the current social contract is meant to disintegrate. If a human body would operate from the premise of *divide et impera,* it would die within a short period of time. The collective body operating from this premise is dying a slow death and now rapidly disintegrating: again, not because of a moral judgment but simply because it cannot sustain life.

Within the Grid, death is seen and perceived as an immutable occurrence or as a rigid sentence by a separate entity or force called God, Allah, and other names. In the realm of Oneness consciousness and universal Laws, death is simply formlessness, the creation of emptiness in preparation for new life, potentially in sync with the pulsations of the Heart and the vibration of Love.

The collective body operating from the premise of divide et impera *is dying a slow death and now rapidly disintegrating: again, not because of a moral judgment but simply because it cannot sustain life.*

The *divide et impera* agreement rests on the separation of mind and Heart, on the separation of human and divine and, as a result, on the collective low self-esteem and disempowerment. It rests on the collective's debilitating fear of standing on its own feet, on the fear or simply avoidance of the discomfort of self-responsibility. It rests on the fear of the wave of change.

Divide et impera is an agreement to remain separate from the source of life. It is an agreement to remain in the more primitive realm of consciousness, because of a core belief that humans deserve to suffer and are incapable of creating anything other than suffering. And of course this vibration will only be able to create such a reality. As these beliefs are held within the collective, the experiences that it generates will only validate the underlying beliefs. They are a self-fulfilling prophecy.

Denial

Another agreement that feeds the aforementioned agreements held in the current social contract—the Grid—is to remain in denial, to stick one's head in the sand and never question how things are created. It is an agreement never to articulate the unspeakable and to protect secrecy by abiding by the rules of the Grid. It is also an agreement never to accept anything other than mechanistic and mentally verifiable reality. In the name of separation, people agree to always look at individual grains of sand, assuming that they bear no connection to one another—because the lens (consciousness) through which they look is capable of perceiving reality only as separate.

> *Denial is an agreement never to articulate the unspeakable and to protect secrecy by abiding by the rules of the Grid.*

This agreement is sealed by the premise that it is not changeable. From the mind's limited perception, this immutability is the only way that safety, trust, and reliability can be experienced. This mindset permeates the collective consciousness and dictates in concrete ways what we perceive as law and how we let ourselves be governed.

Scarcity

Scarce resources are *per se* a consequence of the prevailing collective consciousness held together by the Grid.

Scarcity is a perfect mirror of the Grid consciousness. The premise "there is never enough" emanates a vibration that can only create a daily experience of such reality.

A consciousness that is based on abundance—in more aspects than the mere monetary—sets in motion a vibration that can only generate more than enough. This phenomenon, called many different names, is simple, and we experience it every day. It is a Law that reflects the power of our own unconscious choices, individually and collectively. When we experience it in a beneficial way, it is often considered random or coincidence, rather than the result of an activated co-creative power. When we experience it in a challenging way, it is deemed an unchangeable reality.

Problem Dependence

The lens through which reality is assessed is often limited to a problem. There is a collective agreement to always view an intricate reality not readily decodable by the heart-cropped mind as a problem to which a solution is to be found.

In truth a problem is nothing other than a complex set of circumstances that need to be approached from outside the framework of cropped law. However, the current agreement in the Grid is to approach any circumstances through the mind, which turns them into problems rather than opportunities for innovative co-creation.

In essence, problems exist only within the frame of problem consciousness, where they are continuously perpetuated. The definition of problem itself is one conceived by the mind. The Heart-cropped mind needs a construct that is vibrationally in alignment with the characteristics and *modus operandi* of the mind: a mechanistic analysis of reality.

A problem is a hurdle, a knot that the mind does not know how to untie and penetrate. A problem is an entangled webbing in the throat of an unhealthy body wanting to experience its freedom of expression.

Problem consciousness adopted in the Grid is based in people's perceived inability to manage complexity. It is a cry of desperation by a mind lost in its own limitation in dealing with the unlimited.

Problem consciousness asks for an identification of causes and dissects and separates the elements that presumably contribute to the hurdle. This lens perpetuates the problem. And the solutions emanating from those with such a focus are ones that hold the same vibration. In this sense, such solutions can only call for additional problems, because they are grounded in the same vibrational field.

Viewing a set of circumstances as a mere situation creates space and allows for the grip of the problem consciousness to loosen. The problem approach to a set of circumstances infuses and burdens the situation with beliefs and programs that cloud the vision and hinder the seeing through the veils of the situation. The problem approach thickens the veil and obstructs the essence of the situation, adding vibrational matter that must be processed and diffused. A situation approached from a problem consciousness limits access to the wisdom capable of embracing the whole situation. Such an approach limits access to the breath and space that allows for the wisdom of formlessness to move through the situation.

Problem consciousness is a cry of desperation by a mind lost in its own limitation in dealing with the unlimited.

Problem consciousness solidifies the vibration of the situation and removes the life force that is inherently capable of changing the situation. Problem consciousness is ruled by the mind, which searches for movement while it is based on the premise of immobility.

Problem consciousness cages the situation into the cropped pyramid and therefore is devoid of the creative forces contained in the formlessness of Love. It has limited access to the creative possibilities contained in the whole.

Problem consciousness is ruled by the mind, which searches for movement while it is based on the premise of immobility.

A collective that has agreed to a mind-set operating system espoused to problem consciousness will always finds itself surrounded by a problem-generating machine calling for more problems that create solutions, which in turn cause new problems. It is a collective that has stopped creating and is drowning in its problem of problems. It is a collective that has stopped dreaming, envisioning, intending, and co-creating.

The collective is embedded in the Grid. The Grid in turn is strengthened by the implicit agreement to continuously generate problems that will keep the mind engaged and employed. In fact, the mind will not accept anything other than a problem and a solution within the framework of the problem, because it is not capable of decoding anything other than that which has been generated from its own mind-set.

In this sense, the collective uses its creative power only in that it generates problems and solutions in accordance with the ruling vibration. The collective not only fuels the problem-generating machine at the individual level but also wields its power merely to spawn additional problems and solutions. It perpetuates systems—of governance, law, money, economic, health, and others—that attempt to manage problems by creating additional problems, and generating problem-filled solutions. The collective has entangled itself in a thick web of hopelessness.

> *Once the collective approaches its systemic patterns as situations, a new spaciousness is created that transforms a hopeless problem into a lively possibility.*

Once each being approaches individual life as a situation, and once the collective approaches its systemic patterns as situations, a new spaciousness is created that transforms a hopeless problem into a lively possibility.

Addiction to Suffering and Unhappiness

Closely tied to the agreement of problem dependence is the addiction to suffering and unhappiness. Problems guarantee suffering and unhappiness and serve as an escape route to avoid confronting the devastating fear of having to take responsibility for our own creations.

Any form of suffering and unhappiness calls for Love and compassion, which includes Love and compassion for ourselves as a collective. Encoded in the wisdom of the Heart is the ability to hold the space of compassion while calling forth the power to re-create a situation that frees the individual and the collective from suffering and unhappiness.

However, a new collective choice that presupposes a co-creative power, rather than a victim-oriented perception of reality, is what frees us into a life-affirming vibration. Only when there is a problem are we victims and thus entitled to suffer. When we acknowledge a situation, we are asked to embrace and take responsibility for creating a new situation.

Exhausted by the burden of hopelessness and with an atrophied co-creative Heart, the collective reacts in outrage if asked to embrace its own creations. It is seemingly easier to be victimized by the system, a corporation, a government, a community, or a neighbor. Now is the time to realize that happiness lies in the freedom of a Heart- based co-creation. It is time to realize that the thickness of a problem is thinned and freed by a conscious co-creative act.

Enslavement of Time

Time as currently understood is an ingrained mental concept that has found its way into the cellular matrix of each body, individual, and collective. Time started as a mental construct to alter consciousness into a different vibration of reality. Within the cropped pyramidal structure, time has become a physical expression of limitation: it has become linear.

This mental construct has found its way into the density of the material plane and thus holds reality (reality being defined by the very source of time, being held in the grip of the mental concept of time).

Within the current Grid, we believe ourselves to be locked into linear time. Time is the rabbit everybody is chasing. Time is the pending Damocles' sword that everybody is escaping. Time within the Grid is the container that keeps the masses running, fearing, chasing, blaming, and fighting each other. Time means beginning and end, birth and death. Time is a slight window, a quick breath in a breathless world. Time is the anchor, the last hope and the biggest fear. It is what enslaves us, from the moment when the encodings of linear time held in the collective agreement are released in our bodies—usually within the first five years of life—until our last breath is taken.

Within the Grid, time is what gives us the illusion of identity, as individuals, as a nation. Time is what motivates us as a collective to seek enjoyment, in the realization of the shortness of our lives. Time as conceived in the Grid is the precarious realization of limitation, of the unchangeable container of life, within which to strive and attempt to win what we perceive to be the battle for survival. Time as conceived in the Grid forces us into a futile battle for the best idea that is capable of overcoming time and becoming eternal. This is equally true for individuals as for organizations and nations, which are seeking in vain to win the battle against time and to become perpetual.

> *Time enslavement in our collective has created passive spectators in the* res publica, *a deadening of the responsibility to create the collective systems of choice.*

Individuals and nations are squelched in their ability to meaningfully participate in the weaving of society, because this task in the linear time frame is a lost cause, a time-trapped endeavor we ought to quickly abandon and sacrifice. The futility of this task is a reason to find solace in the quick-fix remedies at the core of our governing structures, cultures, and systems, which are mostly expressions of surrender to the hopelessness of time.

Time enslavement in our collective has created passive spectators in the *res publica,* a deadening of the responsibility to create the collective systems of choice. Time has taken the life force out of our public body. Time has squeezed our collective mind and Heart into machines running on automatic, in desperate cognizance of the enslavement of time. Linear time has turned us into consumers and spectators who passively allow ourselves to be fed ideas devoid of life force, forgetful of the fact that we are co-creators in an organic collective body capable of choosing time.

Cracks and Tears—Window of Choice

The basic matrix in which all life is immersed is a life-sustaining consciousness in which unsustainable life forms are equally embedded. This basic matrix eventually breaks through the most solid and rigid forms of lower consciousness, because life force vibration is always seeking to express itself in new ways. We are collectively at that breakthrough point in time.

The Grid is about to collapse, because it has sustained enough cracks and tears. These cracks and tears are openings, windows of possibility into new forms of life. Which forms are created will depend on the collective's choice. The same power and act of choice that built the Grid in the first place governs any new choices at any given moment. However, if there is an agreement—as in the current Grid—that an act of choice is not even possible, then we remain unconscious of those choices. The possibility at this juncture is to make a conscious choice, a conscious agreement that is life-affirming and sustains the whole, rather than a survival-based agreement founded in a mechanistic view of reality that turns humans into heartless machines fighting each other for scarce resources.

The power that can be unleashed through a collective conscious choice is enormous, and its ripple effects are inconceivable to most, because of the deeply entrenched hopelessness and disconnect that the current collective choice strengthens each day.

Now it is time to awaken to the possibility of a new choice. The Grid is disintegrating because it is not sustained by the core life-affirming cosmic pulsation. This disintegration is triggering a collective anxiety, because a key vibration of the current Grid is the attachment to predictability, a characteristic of a collective ruled exclusively by the mind. In the Grid consciousness, anything that is dark, i.e., unpredictable, unknown, and not identifiable, is intrinsically threatening. However, if the disintegration of the Grid is seen as a window of opportunity for a new collective conscious choice, rather than an overwhelming occurrence that needs to be resisted, the potential for manifesting a smooth and swift transition into a new form of collective self-governance is remarkable.

The same power and act of choice that built the Grid in the first place governs any new choices at any given moment.

Chapter 5

Subtle and Overt Enslavement

Any form of governance is attuned to a certain vibration and level of consciousness. Within any form of governance there are various expressions of the rules adopted at that specific level of consciousness. Currently, we are still dealing with a form of dictatorship: rulership by the few through the enslavement of the masses, or in other words a rulership of the mind.

This form of dictatorship is overt in the case of violent and brutal regimes and subtle in the case of regimes that employ mind control, mass hypnosis, and other means of subjugation.

This form of governance is an expression of the agreements adopted in the Grid.

Propaganda

The word propaganda comes from the verb "propagate"—to spread and disseminate. The seeds of limited consciousness that have been disseminated to this day are falling on the Grid like intermittent poisonous rain. Now we are asked to spread new seeds, new seeds of consciousness, into the web of society.

Propaganda *per se* is a seeding process that has no limiting factors, because it refers to the simple act of distributing seeds, which is a life-affirming expansive act of creation. The determining factor is the quality of the seed, the awareness contained in the seed.

The seed contains the original cell that determines the consciousness of the collective. It is this cell that contains the information, the program of the whole. Therefore, all that propaganda does is to distribute the cells containing the main programming of society. In this sense, propaganda is nothing more than a powerful replication process inherent to the growth and evolution of every social body and collective. It is the process through which a web is formed.

> *Propaganda is nothing more than a powerful replication process inherent to the growth and evolution of every social body and collective.*

As a process of formation, propaganda is neutral and natural. The key is to recognize the power inherent in propaganda, not necessarily as a tool to reach and/or control the masses, but as a natural process of dissemination of the original cells containing the core program of society.

The opportunity now is to dissolve the old unsustainable cells containing Grid-programming and create new cells containing life-affirming and conscious agreements aligned with the vibration of Love.

The first step is to dream, articulate, and then ground the modification of the original cells of society contained in each individual and in the collective body. Contained within these healthy cells is a natural program to propagate—to spread and replicate into the social matrix. So far propaganda has mostly carried a negative connotation, while in fact it has merely been a neutral process of dissemination. What is destructive is the code contained in the DNA, the programs of the cells in the disseminated seeds: the agreements of the Grid.

The freeing and elevation of the collective does not happen through the elimination of propaganda but through the changing of the cells of the collective.

Mind Control

Mind control is not a tool but a description of the quality of the agreements contained in the Grid. It is the very nature of the Grid-agreements that generate mind control. As such, mind control is not an imposed external force. Mind control is intrinsic to the nature of the mind: it continuously controls, battles freedom and spontaneous move-ment, and needs to oper-ate from within a limited environment. Mind con-trol in this sense is prevalent, because in our collective the mind is the lone ruler and as such controls every aspect and face of the collective.

> *Mind control is intrinsic to the nature of the mind.*

Patriotism

Patriotism is rooted in the word "pater"—the father. It is an exaltation and celebration of the pyramidal structure. It is one way individuals express themselves in the collective. It is one way the Grid-cells find ex-pression in the public arena. It is one way the Grid-cells find expression in the pyramid cropped from its foundation.

The values inherent in patriotism are tainted and twist-ed by the grip of the main structure holding together the cropped pyramid—the mind. The values under-lying patriotism are those of loyalty, honor, and love for an entity generated by a trade, a negotiated act by those to whom the power had been delegated in the vibrational band of the Grid. As such, most collective entities like nation-states have for the most part been artificially created by the mind. Within the vibrational band of the Grid, the nation-state is an entity having characteristics, sets of beliefs and programs in accordance with the cropped pyramid.

And patriotism is the call of a twisted form; it is the call of an entity calling out for wholeness; it is the call of a twisted form attempting to assert itself because of the unconscious awareness that it is resting on shaky ground—a pyramid without foundation—a tree without roots—a form desperately trying to conceive itself solely from a father, without the egg and womb of the mother.

> *Patriotism is the call of a twisted form attempting to assert itself because of the unconscious awareness that it is resting on shaky ground.*

Analogically, patriotism tries to breathe life into a form that cannot sustain life but that is being programmed to be the only way of organizing. Patriotism keeps huffing and puffing into that form, unconsciously aware that the form can dissolve any time, because the national entity is an unsustainable form of life. The nation-state, as currently conceived, dwells at the precipice, and those wanting to sustain this form feel the extreme vulnerability of this position and understandably hold on tightly to the edge.

The motivation inherent in patriotism is the desire for a solid foundation in the form of land and in the form of values. Thus at its core, patriotism seeks a whole form. At its core patriotism contains the whisper of liberation. It recognizes at an unconscious level the need for a collective entity to operate in a pyramid grounded in the circle, rooted in the darkness, in the unknown factor, in the Earth. It recognizes the need for a collective form grounded

The life-sustaining vibration in which a nation-state thrives is the one that has anchored its mind in the Heart.

equally in the father and the mother. Patriotism unconsciously recognizes the call to evolve into "patromaterism"—which celebrates, loves, and honors whole forms, whole entities gathered around their own specific land, values, and intentions while being aligned with the fundamental vibration of Oneness consciousness.

In the current vibration of patriotism, the values and intentions honored and celebrated are trapped in the self-destructive and enslaving pattern of the Grid. This entrapment is causing the nation-states and other collective entities to spiral endlessly downward, fighting for their own survival. Collectives unconsciously recognize that their own nation-states or other collective entities dwell in a cropped form and as such do have to struggle for survival, because the only life-sustaining vibration is Love, from which the cropped form is mostly disconnected.

The life-sustaining vibration in which a nation-state, a collective entity, thrives is the one that has anchored its mind in the Heart, the one that has anchored its pyramid in the circle, the one that is anchored in the Earth.

War

War has many forms. The distinction between war and the natural cycle of disintegration lies in the intervention. War is dissolution, with the intervention of a mind disconnected from the Heart space. Disintegration is dissolution generated by the intelligence of the Heart.

War is prevalent, because it is a consequence of the Grid consciousness. The agreements of this old social contract create perpetual war. War is the lone ruler—the mind—at war with itself. In the frame of duality, the mind is always battling the "other." A collective based on the fundamental premise of duality is always trying to define itself with reference to the "other" and perceives differences as a fundamental threat to its own survival. Each individual to some degree is at war with himself and mostly with his own shadow, with the unknown and the indefinable.

> *War is dissolution, with the intervention of a mind disconnected from the Heart space. Disintegration is dissolution generated by the intelligence of the Heart.*

The collective is an accurate reflection of the battles of the mind within human nature. Within the premise of duality, human nature becomes a dependent child. Within the premise of Oneness, human nature becomes an adult. And, within our Heart-based co-creative nature, war becomes obsolete and moot.

In a collective that has let go of the assumption of scarcity, the assumption that everything is a problem to battle, the assumption that everything and everybody is separate and fighting for survival, the assumption that all is invariable … in a collective that has awakened from denial, war is short-lived.

A collective that questions and reflects on the premise and underlying assumptions of each war, a collective that has filtered through and grounded in the Heart data gathered by the mind, will probably recognize war as an outdated and highly ineffective tool of co-creation. Not only will a collective that has awakened from denial see behind the curtains where wars are planned, orchestrated, and propagated into the mass consciousness, but it also will not have even delegated its power to "declare war." It will be a collective that owns its power to create sustainably.

A collective that has filtered through and grounded in the Heart data gathered by the mind, will probably recognize war as an outdated and highly ineffective tool of co-creation.

What about situations that involve brutal dictators and rulers? Is not war the only way to stop the brutality and protect civilians in the name of Love? An empowered citizenry does not need a dictator or a ruler, less so a brutal one. A collective that has let go of Grid-based agreements and is living a conscious social agreement fundamentally in alignment with Oneness conscious-ness creates a vibrational environment in which wound-ed rulers succumb in their own field of desperation and lose the legitimacy to rule.

Again, the level of consciousness of a collective is re-flected in who is leading it. Within the frame of a new social contract, the concept of leadership *per se* is mor-phing into a balanced interplay of leadership qualities in an Earth-grounded pyramid resonant with the wisdom teachings of the Heart. Within this evolved social frame, power is not delegated, and each individual holds the level of responsibility and co-creation correspondent to his own experience and versatility in the field of Love. Each citizen holds the responsibility to co-create in cor-respondence with her ability to translate the needs of individuals, and those of the community, through the Heart Brain. Each individual holds the responsibility to generate creative forms attuned to the ever-changing needs of the community, as opposed to rigidly struc-tured forms characteristic of brutal regimes.

Within the new social contract, groups of individuals are in charge of areas in which they possess Heart Mind competence, and they form creative circular fields within the pyramidal vector of the collective intention, attuned to Heart consciousness. The collective thus creates a vibrational field that reflects Heart-centered leadership.

A collective held together by the agreements of the Grid generates a leadership reflective of the specific vibrational fields brought about consciously and unconsciously by its collective. Brutal rulers can emerge only where the vibrational environment is conducive to that particular form of leadership and where the agreements of the Grid are strongly activated, due to societal patterns and cellular programming of that particular collective.

Diplomacy

Diplomacy is a more sophisticated form of war. As currently practiced, diplomacy is still rooted in the same entangling pattern of the Grid. Behind the veils of even well-intended diplomacy there is often an

> *Diplomacy is a more sophisticated form of war.*

open war, a battle that seeks to determine whose interest and values will prevail.

What determines a collective action is the underlying intention fueling the action. The intention as expressed in the current collective form is entangled in the vibration of the agreements of the Grid. The collective form is the externalization of the shared agreements that unconsciously created the collective intention.

There is a slight difference between individual intention and collective intention. The individual intention is more easily detachable from the Grid, in that it detaches as much as 65% through the act of individual choice. The collective intention is more closely interwoven with the Grid and detachable to a lesser degree (a maximum of 10%) through the act of collective choice.

The malleability of the intention from the Grid determines the range in which a collective act in the current Grid can be effective.

The malleability of the intention from the Grid determines the range in which a collective act in the current Grid can be effective. In this sense, even a diplomatic act of a group or collective that is grounded in the Heart and Oneness consciousness can be only nominally effective within the operating system of the Grid. Within the range of diplomatic acts, most generate directly from within the Grid, and few are grounded in Heart and Oneness consciousness. But even those grounded in this way are at most 10% effective.

The question arises how a collective choice ever detaches from the Grid. It does when enough individuals within their own selves embrace a new collective agreement, because the range of detachment from the Grid for individuals is much higher. Most often the intention of a group that is aligned with Oneness consciousness but is not anchored in the individual intentions of its members is substantially decreased in its effectiveness. Intention formed in this way can only detach from the Grid as much as 10% and thus cannot cause any notable change. However, when the individual and group intentions are aligned with Oneness consciousness, then the collective act becomes fully detachable from the Grid.

This range of effectiveness of combined individual and group intention is rare. The first step toward a fully effective collective choice—effective as to its sustainability and alignment with the new social contract grounded in Love—is a new choice within the individual. The more aligned the individuals in a group, the higher the effectiveness of the collective choice within the group. And the more groups are *fully* aligned with the new social contract, the higher the degree of detachment from the Grid—which, eventually devoid of life force, will disintegrate.

There are two keys to effecting this transformation. One is that the collective needs to be keenly in touch with the purity of its intention. Often the hurdles that block effective intention are left unspoken. Because of the ego-based need to perform as a group in the name of a specific value, and because of a deep pattern of denial and discomfort in approaching the shaky field of human vulnerabilities, it is only once those vulnerabilities are embraced and acknowledged with transparency that the collective act can contribute to a new social contract. The vector of the group intention is weakened by the lack of transparency of individuals in the group and by how this lack is managed and encouraged as a group.

The collective must focus its creative process on aligning with Oneness consciousness, rather than on the disintegration of the Grid.

Transparency has direct impact on the strength of the vector of intention and is a key ingredient to the explosive effectiveness of collective acts and the critical mass that collapses the Grid.

Another key is that the collective must focus its creative process on aligning with Oneness consciousness, rather than on the disintegration of the Grid. This disintegration happens automatically; it is a natural consequence of co-creative forces diverted into a new social contract. Many groups focus their intentions and creative processes on the disintegration of one or another aspect of the Grid, and thus perpetuate the life force contained in the Grid. It is time to focus the collective intention upon the creation of a new social contract.

Chapter 6

Avoidance or Awakening

When the level of consciousness of the collective raises, a new form of governance can be adopted to reflect the maturation of consciousness. When the collective is composed mainly of young children seeking a firm parent and incapable of making independent choices, then overt or subtle dictatorship is a natural consequence. When enough adults comprise the collective, then true governance can emerge.

The passage from childhood dependence into adulthood independence has been a gradual one. And the collective consciousness is now at a point of choice. Many children are still screaming for their fathers and terrified by the prospect of independence. Many adults are also awake to their collective power. And, most of us are confused teenagers who are wondering who we are.

Most of us are confused teenagers who are wondering who we are.

The collective awakening and subsequent emergence of true governance will depend on the inner and outer choices of the many teenagers in our collective. It will depend on our courage to step into adulthood, into emptiness, into freedom and full and mature responsibility for our own choices. It will depend on our willingness to reclaim our power of choice and the power of our compassionate Hearts. The step into adulthood takes courage. No more blaming the parents, and no more hiding out in powerlessness and hopelessness. Awakening is the victory of Heart-centered choices. It is the victory of independence; it is the song of true freedom.

Part II

New Social Contract:
Founded in the Heartland

Chapter 1

New Governing Principles: Unknown Factor and Heart Wisdom

Unknown Factor

The unknown factor is the sacred container of pure potential and possibilities that taps into the matrix of our ever-evolving consciousness. It is the formless space of Love from which true governance and Law can emerge. It is the space of formlessness from which whole forms, whole systems can emerge. It is called unknown because it is foreign to the mind. Embracing the unknown factor as a collective is an act of trust in our true essence as co-creative beings. It is an act of trust in our ability to create a benign world woven together by understanding, compassion, and cooperation.

Heart Wisdom

Heart Wisdom cultivates the understanding of life patterns through the lens of the Heart. It approaches questions of Law, economics, and governance that are basic to all other questions through the keen eye and ear of the Heart.

The truth is that many people's Hearts have shrunk and atrophied through pain, shame, hopelessness, resentment, and blame. Our Hearts have shrunk in our ability to let Love consciously flow through the veins and arteries of our bodies. Accordingly, the flow of Love has dramatically decreased in the veins

Heart Wisdom cultivates the understanding of life patterns through the lens of the Heart.

and arteries of our public systems. They have been drained by greed and scarcity, control and manipulation. When we reclaim the flow of Love within our individual bodies and the public body, balance is nurtured.

Heart Wisdom is the expression of the teachings of the Heart, the vibrational teachings of co-creation and grounded power that have been relegated to the discretionary and segregated realm of religion and spirituality.

Values

The question arises whether the way Love is translated into concrete actions is dependent on the underlying values: Love means a different set of actions, depending on the values each person holds. Could this open the space to arbitrary ways of governance?

The distinction between values and Love is an important one. Values originate in the chamber of the Heart and yet are intimately connected to the chamber of the mind. Values are concepts of the higher mind translated into human awareness by a set of emotions that at times, but not always, originate from the higher wisdom of the Heart.

The distinction between values and Love is an important one.

What keeps Heart Wisdom and values separated is often a distorted translation, resulting from unprocessed emotions from the Grid that cloud access to the higher wisdom of the Heart. This distortion causes values to remain ungrounded. It is only when values land in the Heart chamber that they are grounded and capable of being manifested into life-affirming expressions. When values are freed of the emotional baggage, they are in resonance with the vibration of Love. Then, values are expressions of Love.

Love is the core vibration from which values emanate. Values are the higher mind-Heart translations of human needs. Values are the specifications of Oneness in an understandable, and for the human brain, decodable language. Because values are translations, they are highly susceptible to misinterpretations that result in a disconnection from the chamber of the Heart and consequently in the misuse and manipulation of their essence. The language of unconditional Love is simple, essential, still, clear, and pristine. Its authenticity can be easily read and detected by the brain and muscles of the Heart. This language has been silenced in the law and in our systems of governance. It has become an alien language that the bodies of law and governance are not capable of detecting, reading, and interpreting. It is through the unlocking of the Grid that the com-

The language of unconditional Love has been silenced in the law and in our systems of governance.

munication waves of Heart Wisdom capable of reaching those bodies are unleashed and able to flow once again into our systems. And, the unlocking of the Grid will also make it safe for individuals to trust this new collective communication.

Chapter 2

Unlocking the Grid

The collective consciousness has been held imprisoned for thousands of years by a collective choice. The vibrational current has now changed, creating cracks and tears at the various intersections of the Grid of control.

The cracks and tears are due to the raising of consciousness at the individual level, and due to focused group intentions and rituals. Through these conscious choices, the opening of the cosmic gates of Earth has led to an increased inflow of the Oneness consciousness web to touch, and in certain locations to intersect with, the control Grid. However, the complete unlocking of the Grid requires a collective conscious understanding of the Grid, while currently the majority of people have only an unconscious awareness of it.

> *The unlocking of the Grid requires a collective conscious understanding of the Grid, and a collective choice to surrender and embrace the unknown factor.*

The complete unlocking also requires a collective choice to surrender and embrace the unknown factor. This choice is faced with the greatest resistance. Most—and even many who intend this unlocking— are not willing to live with the uncertainty of what life would be without the control Grid. But when enough individuals and organizations come together with the intention to unlock the Grid and embrace the unknown factor, the cracks and tears will deepen and allow a full disintegration.

Chapter 3

Conscious
Collective Agreements

The new social contract is not a contract as we commonly interpret this word on our plane of consciousness. A contract as understood within the Grid requires a solidification of given circumstances. The new social contract is a common understanding of the fundamental values of society. It is the collective's common understanding of the *modus operandi* of society that allows for the unknown factor to determine, in each given circumstance and moment in time, forms and systems that are moving with the evolution of consciousness. The new social contract is an understanding of the principles of how whole sustainable collective forms and systems are created, and continuously recreated. It is an understanding of how to maximize the life force contained within collective forms.

The new social contract is an understanding of the principles of how whole sustainable collective forms and systems are created, and continuously recreated.

53

The new social contract is also an understanding of how not to take ourselves and our creations too seriously and to lighten up. At its essence, the new social contract is an understanding of how to be in joy rather than in consistent resistance and contraction. It is an understanding of how to reclaim the possibility that life on this planet can, after all, be fun. It is an understanding that life on this planet is not necessarily a *Via Crucis* but a journey of beauty, a path that honors all relations,

The new social contract recognizes the importance of differences as creative ingredients in the container of Oneness— which is Love.

that honors both the commonalities and the differences of each individual and each collective. The new social contract is a new operating system for many collateral systems that each generate their own content and priorities.

The new social contract does not seek to eliminate differences. It recognizes the importance of differences as creative ingredients in the container of Oneness— which is Love. It recognizes each human being, at his essence, as more than a random act of creation.

Oneness and Duality

We can define this new agreement in two ways: including Oneness into duality or including duality into

Oneness. Both are equally important in the collective: the capacity for integrating the whole into the civic dual discourse and for integrating duality in the discourse of Oneness.

In the current Grid, systems, governance, civic and public discourse are founded on the premise of linear "either/or" thinking and are incapable of capturing the complexity of the paradox of the "both/and" that originates in the Heart Brain.

Is duality contained in Oneness? Not necessarily. Incorporating duality into Oneness requires a conscious choice. It is like choosing a lens. Which lens is used in any given moment? The lens of duality? The lens of Oneness? The lens of Oneness that includes duality? There is a precision required in the act of conscious choice, in the act of intention that builds the new collective agreements.

The "Oneness duality" agreement is the vibrational translator of all other agreements. It is the decoding agreement that translates the language of consciousness into a living conscious collective agreement. Oneness consciousness cannot be readily captured. It dwells in the chambers of the Heart, and its vibration is difficult to slow down to the vibration of the spoken word.

Sounds are the words of Oneness consciousness: thus the importance of consciously including music and sound into the weaving of new collective agreements and into the weaving of new systems of governance. Sound is the vibration that grounds the web of Oneness into the plane of consciousness we are operating from, and so it can and needs to be included.

It is also equally necessary to translate the vibration of Oneness into a language of spoken words: words that flow from the sound of Oneness. In this sense, the Oneness duality agreement is a vehicle to slow down the vibration of Oneness into words that can be articulated. It refers to listening to the sound of Oneness and to articulating the words that flow from these sounds. It is an agreement to expand the source of language from one that primarily originates in the dual mind into one that originates in the Heart and is translated into spoken words by the dual mind.

A collective that agrees to this new expanded language is not only one that is capable of articulating complexity in simple terms, but also one that lifts the vibration of the whole with each word.

A collective that agrees to this new expanded language is not only one that is capable of articulating complexity in simple terms, but also one that lifts the vibration of the whole with each word. It is the cumulative effect of this expanded language that elevates the collective and the civic and public discourse. It is this expanded language that makes the collective more prone to connect to its power of self-governance.

From another perspective, this agreement pertains to a new awareness of the far-reaching impact of language. It is an agreement to honor the many ways of thinking about and articulating our differences from within the framework of unity where, regardless of the differences, the collective is woven in a complex web of interdependence. This web, when embraced and grounded in Oneness, creates harmony. When anchored in separation, however, this web is still united and interdependent but creates dissonance and discord.

Variability

A key premise of the new social contract is that it is variable. Variability is intrinsic to life. Variability triggers responsibility. In-variability causes stagnation and eventually enslavement. Variability causes individuals and collectives to create, act, and mold the living collective body, rather than crying in desperation at a dysfunctional and dying collective body.

> *Variability triggers responsibility. Invariability causes stagnation and eventually enslavement.*

Variability is a process, not a value. Values are ingredients added to the living collective body, which is formed and changed by the hands of the citizenry. The variability of the new social contract is not related to the ingredients, but it is the very process of collective creation. Understanding variability means understanding the pulsating of the collective Heart Body. When variability is consciously understood as a value rather than a pro-

> *When variability is consciously understood as a value rather than a process, then the pulsation of the collective body gets out of sync with the vibration of Law and Heart Wisdom.*

cess, then the pulsation of the collective body gets out of sync with the vibration of Law and Heart Wisdom. It is like expecting blood—the ingredient—to fulfill the function of the circulatory system, which is the pathway through which the body pulsates.

Variability is space. It is the space that the collective owns and from which it decides what is important within a society and what content to create. Many collective agreements—such as international conventions, treaties, and constitutions—contain provisions as to their modifiability, but often with high hurdles. This creates stagnation not only with reference to possible new content but also to current content. The vibration contained in those documents then lowers, and then the content loses its effectiveness and the

underlying values drain. The power of such fundamental agreements dissipates. At the root of this dis-
sipation is the assumption that the operating system
underlying constitutions and other governing treaties—the unconscious social contract—is invariable.

When the variability of this underlying operating system upon which constitutions and other fundamental
governing agreements are founded is consciously re-
claimed, these texts are called out of stagnation and
impasse. Then, they once again become living collective bodies, and their past content and values are freed,
opening the door to new living content.

Freedom

A new understanding of freedom is fundamental to
the new social contract. Freedom under the new social contract is radically assumed, not fought for. It
is not a right, because as
such it is presumed to be
negotiable. It is inherent
in every individual and
generates from within the
Heart. Freedom is uncon-
ditional. Freedom is not
circumstantial and exter-
nalized, but an internal-
ized state of being, individually and collectively. It is in
the frequency of Love where freedom is experienced.

> *Freedom is*
> *unconditional.*
> *Freedom is not*
> *circumstantial and*
> *externalized, but an*
> *internalized state of*
> *being, individually*
> *and collectively.*

As such, freedom is not in a state of conflict between the individual and collective spheres; rather, it honors both equally.

Within the agreement of Oneness and duality, freedom is capable of being conceived and lived in the paradoxical and complex space of the Heart as total individual and total collective freedom. A choice between the one and the other does not become necessary, and they can harmoniously co-exist.

Freedom conceived and lived in the Heart space is per se *responsible freedom aligned with the well-being of the whole.*

Freedom from within the dual separated space of the mind is an irreconcilable battle between individual and collective freedom. Freedom conceived and lived in the Heart space is *per se* responsible freedom aligned with the well-being of the whole.

Heart Freedom does not perceive limits. It continually, creatively engages from a contracting and expanding reality and reinvents itself, redefining the frame from within which it wants to express itself.

The role of the new citizen is to listen to the vibration of Heart Freedom, rather than limiting freedom with our own notions of what freedom is. The key is to set freedom free and allow it to express itself within us.

Freedom—although inherent in every citizen—cannot be "owned," because it has its own life. We are simply vessels through which freedom can be expressed. Although freedom can never be robbed of its essence, it can be caged by the mind. Freedom is now calling the collective to be set free, and the key is in the Heart of every citizen.

The role of the new citizen is to listen to the vibration of Heart Freedom.

Responsibility

Responsibility has long been lost. Responsibility has long drowned in the Grid. Responsibility has long been delegated, externalized to family, circumstances, destiny, the system, the government, the "other"— anything but to the self. Even those who celebrate self-responsibility as a high societal value are, from within the vibration of the Grid, still delegating and externalizing responsibility.

Embracing responsibility is what transforms the child citizen into an adult citizen.

But what is responsibility in this new social contract? It is the conscious realization of the power inherent in co-creation. It is the conscious awareness of the power inherent in the self and the collective—whether expressed consciously or unconsciously. Responsibility is a call to awareness of the hidden and open powers of co-creations, such as societal agreements and systems. It is the awareness of the power of the Law which, when left unconscious by the majority of the collective, randomly creates from any place where it is most energized—mostly from within the space of unconscious beliefs and programming originating from the Grid.

> *Embracing responsibility is what transforms the child citizen into an adult citizen.*

Responsibility is an act of awareness through which the source that generates the social contract is diverted from the unconscious (the Grid) to the conscious (the Heart).

> *Responsibility is a call to awareness of the hidden and open powers of co-creations, such as societal agreements and systems.*

Responsibility that is lived from the space of the Grid is muddled and lost. Responsibility that is lived from the space of the Heart is clear and embraced. Responsibility that generates in the Heart is conscious and therefore recognizes the full spectrum of the citizens' co-creative power.

Responsibility within the new social contract means that individuals can no longer blame the government, corporations, an ethnic group, the system, the "other," but are to embrace their power to create what they intend. Thus, at its core the new social contract creates a system that is self-governing: when groups of citizens come together, they do so not with an intention to fight the "other," an external entity or a problem; rather, they gather to creatively bring forth a new form, with full awareness of their co-creative power. In this sense, responsibility is elevated from a mere value to a Heart-centered citizen practice, anchored in the new social contract.

> *Responsibility is elevated from a mere value to a Heart-centered citizen practice.*

Another face of responsibility as lived in the current Grid is expressed in the form of guilt. Responsibility can be elevated when guilt is released. The closest that the collective comes to acting from the Heart is when it acts "responsibly" out of collective guilt. Guilt is only partially anchored in the Heart, in that it is a mind-twisted form of compassion. Collectives that act from this twisted source can only co-create unsustainable collective forms. When the belief underlying guilt is released, compassion can emerge, and collective action can result in whole collective forms.

Responsibility in the new social contract is also the responsibility of those living outside the frame of the mere day-to-day survival to actually choose a new social contract. It is the responsibility of those who more readily have access to the awareness that the door of the cage is open and thus carry the responsibility to actually fly through it. It is the responsibility of those who can see to open the way for those whose gaze, for various reasons, is still focused on one bar of the cage. It is the collective responsibility of those living in comfort to elevate the vibration of the whole by

> *It is the collective responsibility of those living in comfort to elevate the vibration of the whole by embracing the teachings of the Heart.*

embracing the teachings of the Heart and the opportunities it opens.

Balance of the whole is created through new collective agreements, rather than through disjointed collective acts of saving the "other." Balance of the whole is created when the responsibility to collectively, consciously co-create is accepted and expressed through being and living the new social contract. It is not lived by blaming the "other" or by guilt-ridden conditional acts of support. Collective responsibility that originates in the Heart creates a society that is creative, self-reliant, and equally supportive of the self and the whole.

Equality

In the context of the new social contract, equality is a vibrational scale that determines how each collective choice impacts the balance of the whole. Equality is a compass that tips in the direction of Oneness and of the collective, which chooses according to the parameter of the Heart. Equality is a geometrical, collective instrument that is used to balance the whole.

Equality has been misunderstood and interpreted through a too-narrow lens of consciousness. Equality is commonly understood as a right, as a human condition, a measuring factor that discriminates, discerns essence. Equality in the new social contract is a balancing instrument in the hands of the collective, to fine tune creations and attune them in a way that the vibratory infusion from the Heart reaches into the furthest branches of the collective web. Equality is the instrument that ensures that blood reaches to the far endings of each blood vessel of the collective body.

In the societal web there are many different vibratory signatures, colors, and frequency bands. Equality in the web of Oneness consciousness, i.e., in the new social contract, invites each citizen to create according to her own range of possibility and vibratory band. Equality is the compass accessed

Equality is an intricate process of alignment emanating from the Heart Brain.

by each citizen, group of citizens, or nation that has created a collective form or system to balance and align the various frequencies to create a harmonic web.

Equality is an intricate process of alignment emanating from the Heart Brain—the source of formlessness—capable of capturing the harmonics of complexity. Equality, as it has been long understood, is founded on the premise of separation, of disconnected wisdom where each being needs to fight for his own survival. In the new web, being Is, has Been, and always will Be.

Equality in the new social contract presupposes a co-creative power that is exercised at will, consciously generating individual and collective forms that emerge from the Heart. These forms are harmonized by the compass of equality.

Power

Within the context of the new social contract, power is internalized and expressed in alignment with Heart Wisdom.

Power can be perceived through many lenses and within the Grid has mostly found expression through the tight passage at the top of the pyramidal structure of society. Within the Grid, power is an external dynamic, vertically exercised by the various entities along the vertical line of the cropped pyramidal structure of the world order, at the level of nations, groups and organizations, families, and the self. The structure of power is the same in all instances; what changes is the context.

Within the pyramidal structure, the vibration of power is shriveled and fed exclusively by the dual mind. As such, power expresses itself solely through the filters of the beliefs set in the dual mind, which in turn is fed information and programming from the Grid.

The vibration of power—strong and fiery in its nature—is castrated in its current expression, and because of its entrapment in the geometry of the pyramid, it often becomes destructive. The entrapment is generated by what is currently fueling power—the mind—and is continuously strengthened by actions reflecting the mindset of the Grid. This entrapment is also strengthened by architecture: symbols, sculptures, and monuments, all representing the cropped pyramidal structure. These forms then find expression in our systems of governance. In this geometrical shape, power is kept caged to rage.

The vibration of power is castrated in its current expression.

Within the context of the new social contract, power is freed from the pyramid and allowed to flow to its foundation: the circle, the Earth, the people. Power is not limited to the few, but available to the whole. Each individual, each collective is choosing to partake in the expression of the limitless nature of power, each to the degree he chooses.

In the new social contract power is released of moral judgment and opened to express itself beyond the tight confines of domination, which represents only a small fraction (around 5%) of what power is. Within the new social agreement there is an intention to explore power beyond the 5% mark equally within the self and within the collective.

Within the new social contract, power means alignment with the creative source that generates galaxies, star systems, planets, and the Earth. In the process of creating and living the new social contract, power means drawing on the alchemy of the archetypal elements: power being the element of fire, freedom the element of air, responsibility the element of earth, and creativity the element of water. Power means weaving the archetypal elements together by the Love and compassion of the Heart Wisdom teachings.

> *In the new social contract power is released of moral judgment and opened to express itself beyond the tight confines of domination.*

From an alchemical standpoint, current systems are fire-locked within the pyramid, by destructive fire which at best attempts to include the other elements—freedom, responsibility, and creativity. In our current systems, air, earth, and water are ruled by the fire element and locked into the dual mind. Thus, these elements can express themselves only within the context of the dual mind. In other words, freedom can be expressed only as the fight for freedom; responsibility can be expressed only toward the codes and rules set within the cropped pyramid; and creativity can be only minimally expressed, as water can barely flow within an unyielding structure.

Power in the new social contract refers to the awareness of the self's ability to influence and create systems —of governance and other collective forms. It is the awareness of the Law out of which power is activated. It is the expression of the

From an alchemical standpoint, current systems are fire-locked within the pyramid.

spark that starts the engine of our visions of governance. It is the sustainable fire that is not caged and spinning out of control but tempered by responsibility and led by freedom and creativity.

Power in the new social contract is a collective, generative spark that sets in motion the manifestation of sustainable systems, rather than an overbearing force strangling its own twisted creations.

Heart Wisdom

Heart Wisdom is what glues all conscious agreements together. Heart Wisdom is imbued in all other agreements. All agreements intersect with each other. They are not and cannot be separated; they are interwoven and interdependent. Even the old agreements of the Grid are incapable of being separated, because separation does not exist; it is an artificial construct of the mind.

Power is the expression of the spark that starts the engine of our visions of governance.

Heart Wisdom is the strongest thread that keeps the new social contract vibrating with life force and makes the collective body emanate and radiate health. Heart Wisdom brings warmth, brings the perfect alchemical temperature to blend all other aspects of the social contract into whole sustainable collective forms.

Heart Wisdom is accessed in the silence, in the void, in the emptiness. The unknown factor is the space of emptiness, void, and silence. Thus, Heart Wisdom and the unknown factor are intimately connected. The unknown factor is a gateway to Heart Wisdom. When the unknown factor is severed from the collective consciousness, access to Heart Wisdom is restricted and denied access into our systems. Heart Wisdom can at best only trickle

Heart Wisdom is what glues all conscious agreements together.

through the tight pathways of collective dogmatic programming and beliefs, which are then reflected in our systems.

Heart Wisdom is the ability to pierce through the layers of matter and recognize or feel essence. Heart Wisdom provides guidance to remain in right relation and to balance the individual with the whole.

Heart Wisdom is the knowing of the illuminated mind translated into tangible sensory perception of the knowing in the physical plane. The illuminated mind can be accessed only through the pathway of the Heart, because the Heart Brain and illuminated mind are intimately woven together; they are one and expressions of the same source.

Heart Wisdom is accessed in the silence, in the void, in the emptiness.

In the current Grid, the illuminated mind cannot be accessed, because the path that leads to it—the Heart—is severed and devoid of any legitimacy in the collective systems of governance and law, devoid of legitimacy in the operating systems of our society. Thus, the source that is currently accessed in the building of society is drained of Heart Wisdom, shrunk in its life force, and thus unsustainable.

What is the difference between the illuminated mind and the Heart Brain? The source of both is the same. Source is the void—the visible invisible—the tangible intangible—the clear mystery—the known unknown. The Heart Brain and the illuminated mind both understand this language. It is the universal language of existence.

Illuminated mind and Heart Brain have different frequencies: the former more spacious, etheric; the latter more tangible, with more texture. Human consciousness—because of its current vibratory rate in physical bodies— can enter the realm of illuminated mind only through the Heart. The texture of the Heart frequency grounds the vibratory rate of the illuminated mind. It is a matter of translation of data, as within any operating system. So the difference between the illuminated mind and Heart Brain lies in the way the language of existence is translated. Within human beings, the Heart Brain is readily accessed, while the illuminated mind is tapped into after walking through its portal—the Heart Brain.

The difference between the illuminated mind and Heart Brain lies in the way the language of existence is translated.

Most citizens lock each other out of the source from which sustainable societal forms are created.

In the current Grid, most citizens do not even understand that a Heart Brain exists; thus, they consistently lock each other out of the source from which sustainable societal forms are created. When the collective recognizes the fundamental role of the Heart Brain, genuinely sustainable societal forms are created.

What is the difference between Heart Brain and Heart Wisdom? Heart Brain is the pyramidal consciousness within the Heart. Heart Wisdom is the circular consciousness within the Heart. Both Heart Brain and Heart Wisdom contain the illuminated mind, as the Heart is the hub, the center, the "black hole" from which life originates. The Heart is pulsating source, the source that has chosen to exist. Heart is the understanding of the whole. Heart is unveiled sight. Heart is the humble touch for the vastness of existence. Heart is gratitude. Heart is kindness and reverence for life.

> *Heart Brain is the pyramidal consciousness within the Heart. Heart Wisdom is the circular consciousness within the Heart.*

> *Heart is unveiled sight.*

Security in the Feelings of Reason

Within the cropped pyramidal frame of consciousness, data that informs the collective and rules the systems of governance is exclusively gathered from the mind. Legitimacy is exclusively established by a mechanical linear view of reality—by so-called reason. Reliability is exclusively derived from consequential thought processes, and security is experienced solely within the controllable realm of reason. The seemingly uncontrollable, unpredictable, unreliable, illegitimate realm of feelings—one of the many expressions of Heart

Wisdom—is considered a threat, the beginning and the end of a chaotic, unruly, unpredictable, violent, or even brutal society. *Res publica* originated within this frame of consciousness.

Cor publicum acknowledges the obvious: feelings are intrinsic to human nature and as such have legitimacy. Feelings and reason are equally valid and accessed in the co-creative collective process of governance. Feelings and reason are simply different expressions of wisdom—wisdom accessed from different directions and in vibrationally different and yet complementary languages. In *cor publicum,* reason and feelings are each capable of accessing different data, both equally necessary to bring forth collective wisdom: reason capable of dissecting and analyzing, feelings capable of gluing the seemingly paradoxical into an intelligible and intelligent whole. Reasons strengthened by feelings and feelings guided by reason are the pathways to the Heart Mind, to a wise and mature society pulsating with Law.

In a society where feelings are severed, suppressed, and deemed illegitimate, the expression of feelings is unhealthy. This unhealthy emotional expression results in a collective that is either apathetic or angry and violent, caged in its emotional self-censorship, seeking to fully express itself.

A society where feelings are legitimate and included in the co-creation, implementation, and balancing processes of governance is one that experiences a healthy public discourse, one that is freed from its castrated state of being into full creative expression. It is a society that includes emotions in a mature manner, rather than in a tantrum-like expression; a society that finds mental sanity through emotional intelligence. It is a society that, rather than warring with its own erupting suppressed emotions, has freed itself from enslavement and accepted its whole nature and as a result is capable at last of experiencing peace. It is a society that is no longer immature, confused, and trapped in its reasons, but that finally has shifted into adulthood with the light-Heartedness of a child.

Reasons strengthened by feelings and feelings guided by reason are the pathways to the Heart Mind, to a wise and mature society pulsating with Law.

Embracing Complexity and the Unknown

This collective agreement relates to the conscious recognition that the unknown is a healthy stage in any process of creating a sustainable, living collective body. Whereas in the Grid, the unknown remains unconscious and is experienced as a continuous threat that needs to be controlled and contained, in the new social contract, the unknown becomes a natural and healthy factor of existence that is consciously included in the weaving of society.

In the embracing of the unknown factor, complexity is made simple. Complexity is understood and processed in the space of the unknown. A collective that has embraced the unknown factor is one that introduces silence as a process to generate new collective possibilities and

> *In the embracing of the unknown factor, complexity is made simple.*

forms, one that fosters silence as a practice to listen to Heart Wisdom, the wisdom of the *cor publicum,* the Heart Brain of the collective.

A collective that embraces the unknown is one that has learned to trust the darkness and void because it recognizes it as a source of infinite potential, as the source of simple answers to complex situations, as the space where the Heart-logical seeds to whole complex systems dwell. It is a collective that knows that the unknown Is the field where these seeds exist. It is a collective that recognizes that these seeds are activated through the act of collective intention identified by the Heart Brain. It is a collective that knows that the unknown is the foundation of the illuminated mind translated by Heart Wisdom. It is a collective that is aware that group intention anchored in the Heart and directed into the unknown creates powerful and sustainable collective systems of governance. It is a collective that knows and understands how complexity is translated into workable forms that equally benefit the individual and the collective.

A collective that embraces complexity and the unknown is one that knows how to blend the source of unlimited unmanifested ideas with the source of unlimited manifested potential. It is one that blends the light of the illuminated mind with the darkness of the unknown. It is one that knows that both sources are fueled into manifestation by the collective intention accessed and generated in *cor publicum*.

When we embrace the unknown, we provide the collective Heart with the necessary breathing space to organize the cells of the collective body into health.

When the unknown is resisted, the manifestation process is aborted, bringing about unhealthy forms that are forced by the collective mind rather than generated by the collective Heart Brain and Heart Wisdom—the *cor publicum*. When we embrace the unknown, we provide the collective Heart with the necessary breathing space to organize the cells of the collective body into health.

Transparency

The collective agreement of transparency relates to the capacity and confidence of the collective self to know the unknowable, to speak the unspeakable, to hear the unhearable, and to see the unseeable. It relates to the courage to handle the unlimited. It relates to the courage to pierce through denial and share the deep vulnerability of the collective self, in recognition that the act of transparency strengthens trust and denial diminishes it.

A collective that hides in denial is based on mistrust. A collective that shines in transparency is based on trust. This aspect of the new social contract asks the collective what it wants. Within the Grid, the collective's answer to this question is trust, while it affirms that it is not possible to trust "trust"—thus continuously feeding mistrust. Within the new social contract, the collective's answer is vision, with the implied understanding that trust is a necessary ingredient of a workable society.

In other words, the Grid society focuses on the long-lost dream of trust, chasing what it wants. The Oneness society focuses on manifesting the dream, the vision, relaxed in what it wants. This is the gift of transparency.

Abundance

The word "abundance" contains within it the word "dance." The new social contract moves the collective from the petrified state of scarcity into the state of dance.

What if for a moment we assume that there is enough: enough water, enough food, enough air, enough support, enough freedom, enough love, enough respect ... enough to live sustainably? What if for a moment we assume that we are not here to work every day to create the unconsciously declared never-enough-ness, but that we are here to create and follow our passion and Heart, because we know that we are always supported?

We probably find ourselves shaking our heads and may even get angry at this proposition, because the cropped mind space knows and trusts nothing but scarcity. But what if for a moment we have the courage to assume and live the abundance assumption anyway? What do we have to lose? More not-enough-ness. So there is truly nothing to lose.

The societal belief in scarcity and the logical creation of pervasive scarcity is so deeply embedded within the Grid that it keeps the collective body frozen, caged, and enslaved in its own limitation.

Within the new social contract, the collective has awakened from the doom and gloom of scarcity. It is aware that when the collective Heart has awakened, the natural process of creation and manifestation is activated. A society that has the key—the Heart—to tap into the source of the unknown and the source of the known, into the source of light and darkness, into the source of form and formlessness, and into the very source of how sustainable forms are created, is a society that has stopped begging for abundance and is simply experiencing it.

A collective that is in touch with its own co-creative power is abundant, and it is dancing in its creations. A society that dismisses its own co-creative power struggles and tramples in the midst of its own mis-creations. The choice is ours. It is simple and it starts with the choice of each citizen. How are we living? Are we waiting for abundance, or are we living each moment abundantly? Are we see-ing ourselves as members of a scarce society, or are we living in an abundant society? The first funda-mental step is to start to

> *Within the Grid abundance cannot be understood, because it cannot be decoded.*

see the abundance of our society as it is today. This practice generates a vibratory rate that spins the wheel into abundance, rather than one that locks the wheel into scare-city.

What is abundance? Within the Grid abundance can-not be understood, because it cannot be decoded. It is like a foreign healthy cell in the midst of a pervasive cancerous body: abundance is a foreign non-identifi-able concept. Abundance within the new social con-tract is the continuous flow of creation. It is expressed potential from an unlimited source. It is not the source, but a natural consequence of the source. It is not outcome oriented, but describes a process. It is not erratic or selective, but consistent and pervasive. It is assumed, not chased. It is received rather than given.

Abundance within the new social contract is the continuous flow of creation.

A collective that has adopted this agreement has gained the wisdom to tap into the source and has thus gained freedom.

Choice of Time

Time as conceived within the Grid keeps each individual and collective in a continuous battle against the seemingly never disappearing but always increasingly threatening factor of time. Time within the Grid gradually claims more and more space within the individual and collective psyches. It is an endless and hopeless battle, which throws the collective into a desperate quest to slow time or get ahead of it. Time becomes the ultimate predicament, the ultimate hope, the slippery invisible and ever-present reminder of our limitations. This concept of time has become the ruling power and is held together by a tight collective assumption. The effects of time are equally held together by a tight collective assumption.

Now is the moment to pause. Now is the moment to be bold and have the courage to let go of the assumption of time as it has been held in the last few thousands of years.

A society that has embraced the new collective agreement has let go of the absoluteness and embodied the relativity of time. It is a society that realizes that time as understood within the Grid moves within a specific vibrational band that over six billion people have abided by. It is a society that now chooses again, that chooses a vibrational band of malleable time, a society that chooses a vibrational band of relative time, a society that allows each individual and collective to experience time as in sync with its unique sense of balance. It is a society that realizes its power to navigate between times and experience its own timelessness through an act of choice; it is a society that experiments with time and is freed of the monarchical rule of time; it is a society that has embraced a liberated assumption of

It is a society that experiments with time.

time and allows the pulsation of the collective Heart to find and experience time as a servant of balance; it is a society that has made peace with time and has been released from the strangling grip of time.

Within *cor publicum,* each individual, each collective has agreed to enter a new vibrational band of time, to enter the frequency where time is chosen and invoked to set free the collective creative flow. Within *cor publicum,* the society has chosen to live in free time, rather then in monopolistic time. It is a society that rather than being caged in time slavery has found the spaciousness of choice and awakened to its power to choose.

Trust

Trust is an act of giving, an act of generosity, an expression of unconditional Love. Trust is a comforting field to relax into.

The society wrapped around the Grid is one whose trust has leaked out of its body and systems. It is a society that is perennially contracted, tense, and incapable of exhaling into trust. It is a society that is holding on to its breath, drained and exhausted because it can never relax into trust.

Mistrust is the premise of law, the premise of *res publica,* the premise of the current systems of governance. Mistrust is the web that links a society locked into the cropped pyramidal structure, locked into the mind.

Trust is found in the Heart. A society that denies the legitimacy of Heart Wisdom as the very fabric of governance and Law is a society that makes mistrust the ruling assumption. It is a society that creates systems mostly intended to manage mistrust. It is a poor society wrapped in the dream of misconceived wealth. It is a grabbling society coping with the exhaustion generated by mistrust. It is a society that has never relaxed into Love, a society that has never relaxed into the nurturing field of friendliness.

Although many acts of generosity, friendliness, trust, and kindness are expressed in the Grid society each day, their impact is limited because the resulting vibration is embedded in a field of mistrust held together by the collective agreement of the Grid to mistrust human nature, as reflected in our systems.

Within *cor publicum,* trust is a core operating principle that governs all relations. A society that embraces the new collective agreement empowers each individual and each collective to trust in itself, to trust in its ability to dissolve mistrust, to trust in its knowing of the ineffectiveness of mistrust. It is a society that chooses to set up systems that mirror the deeply held vibration of trust in the knowing that acts of mistrust will soon drown in the pervading vibrational field of trust. It is a society that recognizes that the best protection from mistrust is trust; a society that recognizes

> *Mistrust is the premise of law, the premise of* res publica, *the premise of the current systems of governance.*

that in a field of trust a weapon of mistrust loses its life force; a society that, rather than succumbing to mistrust, stands up to trust; rather than fearing mistrust, looks mistrust in the eyes.

It is a society that recognizes the power of trust to break the illusion of mistrust; it is an adult and loving society that understands the needs of the mistrusting children of society; it is a mature and experienced society that does not give away its power to misbehaving children, but in the awareness of its own power—the power to choose—the power to Love—the power of being connected to the pulsating collective Heart—the power of being guided by Law—is capable of neutralizing mistrust and strengthening the field of trust and its collective agreement of trust.

It is trust that allows society to thrive. It is trust that creates a healthy collective body capable of breathing life force into its systems of governance. It is mistrust that creates a sickish, exhausted, and asthmatic collective body, huffing and puffing into its failing

> *It is a society that recognizes that in a field of trust a weapon of mistrust loses its life force.*

systems. It is trust that frees the creative flow of a self-governing society. It is mistrust that asks for a subtly or overtly dictatorial system of governance. It is a fearful society that creates more reasons to fear each day and shrinks into apathy. It is a loving society that creates more opportunities to love each day and is creatively engaged in governing itself.

A mistrusting society is afraid to choose. A trusting society continuously chooses.

A mistrusting society is afraid to choose. A trusting society continuously chooses. A mistrusting society is ruled by its unconsciousness. A trusting society embraces its unconsciousness and turns itself into a conscious collective being.

Self- and Collective Awareness

Awareness is the basic premise of the new social contract. Awareness is power. Awareness is freedom. Awareness is responsibility. Awareness is abundance. Awareness is Heart Wisdom. Awareness is equality. Awareness is transparency. Awareness is variability. Awareness embraces complexity and the unknown. Awareness is aware of Oneness and duality. Awareness is the practice of the new citizen.

Awareness is found in the silence of the Heart.

Awareness is the ability to remain witness in the unfolding individual and collective story. Awareness is found in the silence of the Heart.

Self- and collective awareness are equally important in the creation of a new social contract. They are interdependent.

Within the Grid, awareness is shunned and considered a threat to the *status quo,* to the rigid cropped pyramidal mind. When awareness exists within the current Grid, it is either focused and hidden in the individual or focused in a specific collective but disjointed in the individuals forming the collective. Rarely is awareness focused in both the individual and the collective, equally and consciously.

Within the new social contract, awareness is balanced within the individual and the collective. One is seen as the reflection of the other. The individual realizes himself in the collective, and the collective realizes itself in the individual.

> *The individual realizes himself in the collective, and the collective realizes itself in the individual.*

Awareness within the new social contract is the choice to be conscious, to be conscious of unconsciousness. It is the choice to create conscious collective agreements. It is the choice to end enslavement and embrace power. It is the dedication and surrender to the wild dance of life. It is the power to finally Be adult citizens.

Chapter 4

Process of Change

How can we bring about these new collective agreements? Within the Grid, we need to know in advance. Within the new social contract, the need to know is surrendered.

Answers are found in the act of co-creation, in the moment of individual awareness and integration of these agreements, in the moment when *cor publicum* is activated through a new collective intention.

What has kept humanity trapped in the cropped pyramidal structure is control—the need to know in advance *how* to bring about a society that operates on new core agreements, *how* to balance individual and collective needs, *how* to make sure that individual freedom is protected and the common good met.

Within the new social contract, the need to know is surrendered.

The key lies in the unknown factor through which the new core agreements are activated. The key lies in the realization that the *how* is continually revealed each step of the way, moment to moment. The addiction to prediction is ended by the embracing of the unknown factor, and the door to a new society opened in the present moment of co-creation.

> *The addiction to prediction is ended by the embracing of the unknown factor, and the door to a new society opened in the present moment of co-creation.*

Within the Grid, society keeps waiting for answers, keeps waiting for the perfect plan, keeps waiting for problems, keeps waiting for solutions. Within *cor publicum,* society acts in the silence of wisdom, acts in the awareness of its power as a co-creative entity, acts in the individual awareness of interconnectedness and in the collective awareness of individuality.

Within *cor publicum,* the *how* is not generated by the cropped space of the mind, by a society always trying outdated, deadened formulas to escape from and cope with the problem. The *how* is generated in the whole space of the Heart Mind, pulsating with solutions and choices that emerge from the individual and collective wisdom. The *how* is generated by a Heart-centered society attuned to the needs and solutions of the present situation.

The process of change is the shift from a coping society to a creative society that trusts that the *how* does not need to be fed from the top of the pyramid—the controlling mind—but is emerging in the unlimited darkness of infinite possibilities beneath the pyramid, accessed by the Heart Mind and articulated by a conscious exchange between the individual and the collective.

Critical Mass

What does it take to change a few-thousand-year-old contract? Change within the premise of variability happens in a heartbeat and emerges consciously. Change within the premise of invariability happens in long, painful cycles and is mostly unconscious.

The first step is to realize that a new choice is concretely available now with each pulsation. The second step requires the courage and boldness to embrace the unknown, to dive into (what the mind considers) uncharted waters, with the knowing that water always lies on level ground.

> *Change within the premise of variability happens in a heartbeat and emerges consciously.*

The third step is to leap, individually and collectively, in that each individual connects to the collective and each collective connects with the individual with internalized power and freedom.

So far, even well-intended individuals and collectives desiring to change the basic social contract interact with the Grid systems from within the Grid agreements, thus bringing about little change. We interact with the Grid, with the vibrational undercurrent of powerlessness, overwhelm, despair, and time enslavement. We interact individually and collectively from the premise of separation, or being "other than."

The key into the new social contract is to become an adult citizen with the light*Heart*edness of a child. The key is to surrender the emotional immaturity and expand mental maturity with Heart Wisdom. The key is to individually EMBODY the new agreements, in the knowing that the collective body—because of its interdependence with the individual—instantly absorbs the embodied agreements. Conversely, the

> *The key is to surrender the emotional immaturity and expand mental maturity with Heart Wisdom.*

key for each collective is to EMBODY the new agreements, in the knowing that the individual body instantly absorbs the new operating system of the collective.

Many desiring to change the social contract still hold the conviction that they are separate from the collective body, thus blocking the vibrational pathway of individual change that ripples into the collective body. The key into the new social contract is to live simultaneously in the awareness of our individual and collective selves. The key is to embrace and embody the knowing that the individual body Is the collective body, that the collective body Is the individual body.

The invariability of the fundamental social contract has been locked for thousands of years by the code of separation. This code can be changed within our individual and collective DNA: from separation to interconnectedness. This process opens the spiral of conscious change. It accelerates and eases the process of disintegration that is already occurring, opening the pathway to the emergence of new, sustainable, mature collective agreements. This

> *The key into the new social contract is to live simultaneously in the awareness of our individual and collective selves.*

"code change" alters the environment of systemic change, transforming the environment from a choppy and tempestuous sea of unconsciousness into a calm ocean of consciousness.

The key into the new social contract is conscious collective participation in holding the vibration, the essence of the new agreements. Again, from within the Grid, many individuals and collectives are holding aspects of the new social contract separate from each other; a concentrated, consistent, congruent, and coordinated intention and embodiment of the new social contract by individuals and collectives in their complete awareness of interconnectedness is still awaiting to unfold.

Within the collective, 2.5% of life consciousness is required to open the pathway to cor publicum.

When the wiring of consciousness is open and clear, when the authentic worldwide web of consciousness is activated and held together by the center—the Heart in each individual and in each collective—the communication of Heart Wisdom—is restored, and the new social contract of *cor publicum* is activated.

This activation occurs in fractal terms: within the individual, the activation of 25% of life consciousness is required to open the pathway to Heart Wisdom; within the collective, 2.5% of life consciousness is required to open the path-

The old social contract holds life consciousness to less than 1%.

way to *cor publicum*. Once the pathway is opened, a wave of consciousness activated to a degree of 125% moves through mass consciousness, and the new fundamental contract of *cor publicum* is awakened to life.

Social contracts each move within a different vibrational band, and each band is connected to a changing percentage of life consciousness. The old social contract holds life consciousness to less than 1% and, therefore, is squeezed into a very thin band of life. As a result, the old social contract is generating forms of governance and systems holding less than 1% of life consciousness and thus perpetuating war, suffering, and continuous despair.

Furthermore, within the vibrational band of the Grid, attempts to shift the social contract are necessarily cumbersome, draining, and often ineffective, because of the lack of vibrational spaciousness. *Cor publicum* holds life consciousness to a degree of 77%, and thus its capacity to generate forms attuned to life wisdom is greatly increased.

Although cor publicum *does not encompass 100% of life consciousness, it still holds the potential of an unprecedented leap.*

Many variations of the old social contract in the last thousands of years have all ranged within the 0–2% range of life consciousness. Even when they were perceived as radical from the perspective of the cropped pyramidal space, these changes were still minor in relation to *cor publicum*. Although *cor publicum* does not encompass 100% of life consciousness, it still holds the potential of an unprecedented leap.

In summary, *cor publicum* is activated in any given fractal of society when 2.5% of collective life consciousness, and 25% of individual life consciousness (of the participating 2.5%), is attuned to and living in Heart Wisdom. *Cor publicum* holds 77% of life consciousness, compared to the 0–2% range of the systems of governance in the last thousands of years.

Chapter 5

New Citizen

It is in the quiet that the teachings of the new citizen are emerging.

The new citizen is the one who has learned to dwell in the silence, in the emptiness of the in-between moment. He is the one who has suspended the intermittent restlessness of the mind, the courageous one who has paused to question and reflect, the one who has integrated the past and is devoted to bringing the dream to fruition in the eternal moment of now.

> *The new citizen has suspended the intermittent restlessness of the mind.*

The new citizen is the one who is pulsating with life and embracing suffering, hopelessness, tyranny, and brutality, and is finding freedom in the acceptance of the many faces of Oneness. He is the one who chooses to see, hear, understand, ponder, re-evaluate, pause, fall into dissolution, and rise into an integrated whole.

The new citizen is the one who dwells in the continuous knowing of the unknown—the one who flows with changes and surrenders to Love—the one who offers herself into the blissful and exalted moment of co-creation. She is the one who speaks with humble assertion of her own limitations—the one who engages with the firmness of her own power and the kindness of her own intentions—the one who is awake and willing to lift the veils of illusions and Be free—the one whose home Is in the Heart.

He is the one who chooses to see, hear, understand, ponder, re-evaluate, pause, fall into dissolution, and rise into an integrated whole.

The new citizen is the one who follows the whispers of his own warrior and has the courage to dwell at the edge of the precipice, at the edge where political identity is dissolved.

The new citizen is the one who dwells at the edge where his beliefs are held and yet grounded into the unknown factor—the one who dwells at the edge between separation and union, between individuality and the common cause.

The new citizen is the one who has learned to live in balance, in between form and formlessness—the one who is the glue that leads formlessness into form—the one who emanates the awareness that holds the governing container—the one who vibrates in freedom and consciously weaves her individuality with the collective—the one who has the courage to Be the Cor—the Heart—of the collective.

> *She is the one who has the courage to dwell at the edge where political identity is dissolved.*

The new citizen is the one who lives in the awareness of Oneness consciousness while traveling to other vibrational bands of consciousness—the one who is whole in his separation—the one who is separate in her wholeness. She is the one who has integrated paradox—who has integrated the simplicity of complexity—who trusts untrustworthiness—who fears in the space of Love and loves in the space of fear—the one who chooses to not decide and decides to not choose— the one who finds comfort in the discomfort and is uncomfortable in the comfort. He is the one who is free from the bondage of limitations and has learned to fly on his own wings in the grounded awareness and in the direction of the whole.

The new citizen is the one capable of holding the whole in her individuality and the one capable of

> *The new citizen is the one who has the courage to Be the Cor—the Heart— of the collective.*

holding individuality in the whole—the one bridging individuality and the collective through the weavings of Heart Wisdom.

Chapter 6

Corporations

Corporations are *per se* neutral, simply one of the many forms of possible collective action. The word corporation contains the word "corpus," or body. It originally referred to a body of individuals. The corporation is a structure, a form that becomes vibrationally filled with life force only with an act of intention. Without an intentional vector to gather around, corporations are lifeless, empty structures. When an intentional vector is formed, a corporation becomes a co-creative entity.

> *Collective hysteria around corporations is an expression of powerlessness of a collective enraged at the outrageousness of its own choices.*

Collective hysteria around corporations is an expression of powerlessness of a collective locked into the Grid; it is the rageful expression of a collective enraged at itself, enraged at the outrageousness of its own choices.

The focal point of these expressions is a war, a battle against a form that is nothing more than a mirror of the collective agreements of the Grid. The fight against the ailing body of corporations keeps the collective embedded in its own disease. It is not the form that has created the imbalance. It is the intention of a form fed and perpetuated by collective intentions, choices, and practices that has created the imbalance.

Corporations do have "personhood" status—if not in the legal sense certainly in the sense of their ability to create. The tension does not arise over whether corporations do or do not have personhood status. The tension arises from the core intention that weaves the organization together and generates action.

Corporations—as is true of other collective forms—become organic living bodies because of the interconnectedness of the form and the individuals comprising the aggregation. A corporation gains its life form directly from the life force of the individuals forming it. In other words, the *corpus* takes on life force of its own once the collective intention of the individuals forming the corporation has gathered enough life force, and once

The life form activation of corpus happens when 45 to 55% of the life force of the individuals is transmitted to the body.

this life force is transferred into the body. Concretely, the life form activation of *corpus* happens when 45 to 55% of the life force of the individuals is transmitted to the body.

Within the paradigm of the Grid, corporations never come fully into life, because the individuals are engaging within this form as separate, disconnected, estranged entities, thus having little life force to infuse into their *corpus:* usually 10 or 15% at the most. As a result, corporations are already weak and in a state of imbalance at their incorporation.

Full incorporation according to Law occurs when individuals forming the corpus *are attuned to life force. This life force is accessed through Heart Wisdom.*

Full incorporation according to Law occurs when individuals forming the *corpus* are attuned to life force. This life force is accessed through Heart Wisdom. Individuals attuned to Heart Wisdom are capable of transmitting into the *corpus* a higher percentage of life force—at least 75%. In other words, a corporation is "alive" and contains life force when it has received a transmission of 75% of life force by its individuals.

Individuals are capable of transmitting life force only if attuned to the Heart Mind. In this sense, *corpus* is fully interconnected with the individuals forming and engaging with it. And corporations *per se* are capable of holding only the vibrational quality held by the individuals forming and engaging with the *corpus.*

The life force field of *corpus* is generated and strengthened in three ways: by those directly engaged in its incorporation, by those working within the *corpus,* and by the community choosing to engage and exchange with the *corpus.*

Within the Grid, corpus *needs laws to find its legitimacy, because it has never received Law at its birth. Within* cor publicum, *individuals and collectives are transmitting life force to* corpus *and thus connecting* corpus *to Law.*

Within the Grid, *corpus* has little life force. It is cropped from the source of life—the individuals—and incapable of holding Heart Wisdom, because the individuals incorporating and engaging with it are operating from the premise of separation. *Corpus* becomes devoid of Heart Wisdom and operates mostly exclusively from within the cropped pyramidal mind frame.

At the core, individuals and the collective are responsible for the essence and quality of *corpus:* if individuals and the collective are not attuned to Heart Wisdom, corporations are *per se* incapable of being more than disconnected, twisted forms lost in the confusion of the mind. They are scrambling to survive and constantly at war with their competitors, all fighting for more life force, fighting for an essence that was not transmitted at inception, and raging or crying before an eventual and inevitable disintegration.

Within the Grid, *corpus* needs laws to find its legitimacy, because it has never received Law at its birth. Within *cor publicum,* individuals and collectives are transmitting life force to *corpus* and thus connecting *corpus* to Law. Individuals create *corpi* that hold and exchange life force, and that reflect Heart Wisdom. In turn, corporations meaningfully contribute to the whole, as amplified and effective generators of collective Heart Wisdom and as effective vehicles that translate into practical forms the operating agreements of *cor publicum.*

Part III

New Governance:
From Res Publica to
Cor Publicum

Cor publicum *is a new form of governance,
a self-organizing principle infused
with a "freed" Law nurtured by
the gentle touch of Love and compassion.*

Cor publicum *is the Heart integrated and
expanded into the new social contract.*

Cor publicum *is created by the conscious
intention of each citizen to live in the
compassionate Heart.*

Cor publicum *is the Heart of the whole
called forth by the collective body.*

Cor publicum *is creative potential
waiting to be chosen to exist.*

Chapter 1

Cor Publicum and the American Declaration of Independence

How does the Declaration of Independence relate to *cor publicum*? The Declaration of Independence was a seed. *Cor publicum* is the blossoming flower.

The Declaration of Independence contains glimmers of the new social contract. Its impact has been far reaching, and yet its content is reflective of the consciousness of that time and thus in need of being freed into the evolving consciousness.

The content of the Declaration is stagnant, while it also has a strong pulsation to erupt into its full expression. This document has been trapped in duality: by those asking that it be brought again to life and by those denying its significance because of its outdated nature. It is now time to free the Declaration from duality, and in recognition of its revolutionary nature it is time to allow it to evolve and fully express its explosive and consciousness-changing core potential.

It is time to draw on the spirit that brought forth the Declaration, while allowing it to evolve into what its authors could not articulate at the time it was adopted. When the Declaration is released from the tug of war, from the battle of beliefs, from the Grid consciousness and into the collective, each citizen can drink from the courage, creativity, boldness, and innovation it contained.

The life force contained in the Declaration can be accessed when it is not rigidly attached to its specific content, when the vibration it holds is drawn to create a new social contract, a new declaration of independence, a new declaration of the radical independence of the self and the collective, a new declaration of co-creative power, a declaration that recognizes *cor publicum* as the gate and source of true independence.

> *The life force contained in the Declaration can be accessed when the vibration it holds is drawn to create a new social contract.*

The Declaration of Independence of 1776 and *cor publicum* are different, in that the declaration is embedded in the historical circumstances and consciousness of the time it was adopted. But they are linked in that *cor publicum* is the continuation, the evolutionary potential of the declaration. Both originate from the same intention to listen to human potential.

In the same way, *cor publicum* is the evolutionary potential of the Great Seal of the United States. The Great Seal enfolded the collective consciousness at the time of the American Declaration of Independence. As such, the Great Seal carried real potential but also the limitations of the Grid.

Both the Declaration and cor publicum *originate from the same intention to listen to human potential.*

The symbols contained in the Great Seal to this day carry layers of entangled meanings, and they determine for most of us unconsciously the blueprint from which forms of governance emerge, well beyond the national boundaries of the United States.

It is the blueprint emanating from the Great Seal that shapes the field of collective consciousness and the forms of governance the collective is capable of generating. It is this blueprint that subtly determines the range and quality of the forms of governance that can survive in it. In this sense, the Great Seal does actually seal the vibrational field of governance, and as such it has far greater influence than we are consciously aware of. And as long as the Great Seal is locked into the Grid consciousness, sustainable forms of

Cor publicum *is the evolutionary potential of the Great Seal of the United States.*

governance within the far-reaching field of the Great Seal remain a quest.

Cor publicum opens the Great Seal and frees the human potential contained in the American Declaration to express itself into an ever-evolving blueprint of governance. Within *cor publicum*, the life force that fuels the field of governance does not originate from a sealed blueprint but from the pulsating collective Heart.

Cor publicum *unlocks the hidden power of the pyramid.*

Cor publicum unlocks the hidden power of the pyramid.

Chapter 2

Wisdom of the Pyramid and Circle Combined

The geometrical field underlying Law—out of which governance emerges—is pyramidal in nature. It is now time to infuse the pyramidal structure into the darkness of Earth, into the unknown. Can we live with the unknown? This is the archetypal value that is in need of being brought to conscious awareness. When the unknown factor is brought into the pyramidal structure, the pyramid starts to spin and find a new sacred shape that resonates with the universal Laws of consciousness.

Law as experienced in *cor publicum* has been brought into secular law to a level of 40%. As we open the space to the unknown factor—the ingredient feeding the roots of Law—the structure becomes alive and whole, and secular law becomes capable of expressing a higher percentage of Law. The pyramid becomes flexible and capable of containing the complexity of human nature and behavior.

> *Law as experienced in* cor publicum *has been brought into secular law to a level of 40%.*

113

The whole and alive pyramid—as opposed to the cropped pyramid—is rooted in the circle. When we operate from the ge-ometry of the circle, an alchemical marriage be-tween the creative forces contained in the circle is set into motion. These creative forces generate a vibrational spin that creates a pyramid that is effective rather than de-structive and that is aligned with the vibration of sus-tainable forms.

From a pyramid grounded in the circle, whole forms of governance emerge—the potential for true justice, freedom, equality, and peace emerges.

We have been living exclusively in a pyramid that is not grounded in the circle. It is our old social contract that has created this unfounded field. As long as the energy is exclusively in the pyramid, in the mind, in the up-per part of the body—only twisted creations doomed to generate pain and suffering and a deep disconnect from the Earth can emerge.

The pyramid at the center of our current society is a forced creation that has a weak vibrational foundation to stand upon. But when we activate the circle—which allows us to tap into the unknown factor—we set into motion an alchemy that naturally creates a pyramid that is grounded in the energy of the Earth and the wisdom of the Heart. From this alchemical space of creation, from a pyramid grounded in the circle, whole forms of governance emerge—the potential for true justice, freedom, equality, and peace emerges. To move from potential to experience, the act of intention and choice is needed.

Chapter 3

Law and Governance

What is Law and what is governance? And how do they relate to each other?

Law as commonly understood within the Grid is an instrument of control and domination used to delegate legitimacy, and along with legitimacy, it is used to delegate power. Law and legitimacy are tied together as a values-based act of delegation of power. Legitimacy is an illusionary mind construct, an illusionary way to control and determine what is beyond control, what already is and always will be, and thus legitimacy is unrelated to Law.

> *Legitimacy is an illusionary mind construct, an illusionary way to control and determine what is beyond control.*

Within *cor publicum,* Law is an organizing principle. It is descriptive and not values based. Law simply Is and always will be and is freed from the analysis of legitimacy. Does a mountain, a river, a volcano, an ocean, need legitimacy to exist? It simply is.

The same principle applies to a system of governance. It does not come into existence because it is legitimate, but because it is decided. Legitimacy given to a government, nation, or ethnic group is a mind-based act of control—or illusionary control. It is an arbitrary

Law simply Is and always will be and is freed from the analysis of legitimacy.

act dependent on a collective that has declared itself in control to "convey" legitimacy.

Law is unconditional and a process of existence that is beyond the understanding of the mind. Law is found in the space of the Heart and does not need to be articulated, but simply keenly observed. Law is not intricate; it is simple, clear like a mountain spring.

Within the Grid, laws are just another instrument to placate ourselves, to distract and prevent us from observing Law and living, creating according to Law. Within the Grid, laws are simply the vibratory match for the state of consciousness of the Grid. If Law were understood, no laws would be

A system of governance does not come into existence because it is legitimate, but because it is decided.

necessary; laws are reflections of the misunderstanding and forgetfulness of Law; laws are instruments of the lone ruler of the mind and continuous reminders of inadequacy.

Within *cor publicum,* Law is expressed Heart essence: within the Grid, laws are desperate ways to grasp power. Law is power. Law is, and as such cannot be delegated. Law is inalienable. It simply applies. It is similar to the unnamable set

Law is not intricate; it is simple, clear like a mountain spring.

of principles and processes that make a physical body function. Law is the expression of source.

Governance relates to collective decision-making. It differs from Law in that it is not an organizing principle *per se,* but it becomes an organizing principle with a specific act of intention—by an individual, a few, or a collective.

Within the Grid, governance defines structures of authority and is mostly based on the premise of delegation of power. And laws are the executors of governance; laws are mirrors of those who govern; laws are content set by those who govern—thus making laws an arbitrary expression of those who have claimed legitimacy.

Laws are reflections of the misunderstanding and forgetfulness of Law.

Within the new social contract, governance is the practical translation of Law. However, for thousands of years Law and governance have been kept separated like two foreign domains. Within the Grid, Law has been replaced by laws. Law in the Grid has been practiced as a translation of governance, and governance has been perceived as the source of laws. This role reversal has caused governance to lose its connection with the full vibratory rate and possibility of true governance. It has caused governance to become a set of structures with no foundation to rest upon. It has caused governance to lose its connection with Law. When governance flows out of Law, governance is in sync with the universal operating system, with the principles that sustain life and whole sustainable collective forms. These forms are then capable of ensuring balance within and among individuals and within and among collectives. Governance thus becomes the structural language of Law.

Within cor publicum, *Law is expressed Heart essence.*

When governance flows out of Law, governance is in sync with the universal operating system, with the principles that sustain life and whole sustainable collective forms.

Chapter 4

Power and Governance

For thousands of years, governance and power have been equated: those who govern are in power, and those who are in power govern. This interpretation of the relationship between power and governance does not do justice to the essence and meaning of power or governance. Power does not flow from a structure. Power can be infused into a structure, but it is not the structure that allows the exercise of power. The structure is not an instrument of power; governance is not the instrument of power either.

> *When each citizen and collective exercises power, a flexible structure expressing Law is created.*

Within *cor publicum*, power and governance are woven together: when each citizen and collective exercises power, a flexible structure expressing Law is created. Power is exalted in the expressions of governance, because power provides a free pathway along which the creativity of the collective is accessed through collective Heart Wisdom and organized in alignment with Law.

Power fuels governance in that it gives governance the organic movement to remain at the service of those who create it—the individuals and the collective. Power keeps governance linked to its source, i.e., to those who access their own co-creative power. In this sense, power prevents governance from becoming a separate, disconnected structure that in time develops its own laws.

Power prevents governance from becoming a separate, disconnected structure that in time develops its own laws.

Power keeps governance in the hands of those who create, rather than taking it away from those who delegate. This is why the exercise of power by each citizen is so crucial in the creation of governance: when power is delegated, governance spins into a self-created, self-serving dynamic; it creates a life of its own, far from the needs and intentions of those whom it is meant to serve. When power is delegated, governance is lost.

When power is exercised, governance retains its essence and remains a sculpture in the hands of the artist. It is a sculpture that can be molded, changed, maintained, preserved, and transformed in sync with collective intention. Exercising power is not an option. It is the main ingredient of how governance emerges.

Authority and Power

Authority is control; power is free. Authority battles; power simply is. Authority comes and goes; power always remains. Authority bends, shrinks, explodes, twists, turns, fights, gasps, screams, and cries, and it is never satisfied; power simply is. Authority struggles for survival; power is eternal. Authority is the illusion of power; when authority is challenged, power simply is.

Exercising power is not an option. It is the main ingredient of how governance emerges.

Authority is the illusion of power.

The systems of governance and the laws within the Grid are expressions of authority. Governments and laws become such because they claim authority. Considering that authority is a mirage, governments and laws are built on sand and thus at their essence are highly vulnerable and continuously

Considering that authority is a mirage, governments and laws are built on sand.

attempting to assert themselves in the awareness of their own precariousness.

Governance that is an expression of power has a consistent and solid—but not rigid—foundation; such governance cannot be challenged, but can simply re-create itself. Such governance does not need to resist, but emerges from an easeful interplay of power, freedom, responsibility, equality, transparency, abundance, and other principles within the new social contract.

Morality and Love

Within the current agreements of the Grid, Love is immoral; Love is a spineless and corruptible principle.

> *Governance that is an expression of power cannot be challenged, but can simply re-create itself.*

Love is threatening, because it is incapable of dissecting life into good and bad and thus untrustworthy. In a mind-ruled society, safety is found in morality, a frame of reference that distinguishes between what is acceptable and what is unacceptable.

Morality is an expression of Love. Yet morality is incapable of vibrating the full spectrum of Love, because it is contrived within the narrow limits of the cropped pyramid, which does not provide the space for Love to express its full essence.

Morality is one expression of the many faces of Love. Love is all expressions.

Morality is Love burdened by the weight of judgment. Love embraces all judgments.

Within the current agreements of the Grid, Love is a spineless and corruptible principle.

Morality punishes. Love is consistent.

Morality screams for integrity. Love silently offers it.

Morality discriminates. Love discerns.

Morality is threatened by Love. Love embraces morality.

Morality is the illusion of safety. Love is protection.

Morality rules *res publica*. Love pervades *cor publicum*.

Chapter 5

Rule of Law

The "rule of law," as developed and interpreted in the past hundreds of years, brought about important breakthroughs in the advancement of consciousness. Yet this principle has remained frozen in the tight vibrational band of the Grid, in that it referred to laws rather than Law. As such it has contributed to the enslavement of the collective.

Within the Grid many well-meant principles, even the few anchored in Law and governance, have created an upward movement in the spiral of consciousness, but because of their entrapment in the Grid they have become stale and have perpetuated the state of enslavement.

> *The rule of law becomes the "rule of Law" when it draws its life force from the formlessness of the Heart space.*

In this regard, the rule of law has been locked in the upper pyramid, becoming a dictatorial order rather than a democratic, compassionate principle to be applied in accordance with Law. The rule of law becomes the "rule of Law" when it is freed in its vibration, when it includes the unknown factor, when it draws its life force from the formlessness of the Heart space.

Chapter 6

Law and Heart

Heart is Law. Law is Heart. Both are intimately connected.

Law is the language of the Heart, the articulation of Heart Wisdom. Heart is the sound and image of Law.

Heart and Law are the language, sounds, and images of wisdom.

At their core, Heart and Law are both transmitting the vibration of source in

Heart is the sound and image of Law.

a slightly distinct manner: Law is the web of creation; Heart is the pulsating infusion that sets creation into motion.

Law and Heart are *cor publicum*.

Law and Heart are cor publicum.

Where Law and Heart are consciously embraced by the collective, a society grounded in matter emerges. Where law and mind are ruling the collective, a society disconnected from matter survives.

Both and all options are available. It is our choice.

Chapter 7

Natural law and Law

Natural law is framed as a sector of law. Law is all encompassing. Natural law and Law intersect in their recognition of the source. Natural law hinted at Law. Law is conscious awareness of existence.

Natural law emerged in a field surrounded by dead crops. Law is emerging in a field ripe for the fruits of wisdom.

Natural law cracked the cropped pyramid to conceive the foundations of society beyond the narrow pyramidal approach of legal positivism. Natural law emerged in a field surrounded by dead crops. Law is emerging in a field ripe for the fruits of wisdom.

Law is the view of the open field beneath the pyramid.

Natural law missed the core pulsating essence of Heart Wisdom, forcing this field into the deadened pyramidal frame of reference. Law is an expression of Heart

Wisdom pulsating eternally and capable of being accessed, transformed, and freed into the collective field when a new individual and collective choice is made.

Natural law peeked through the crack of the pyramid, individuating partial aspects of Law. Law is the view of the open field beneath the pyramid.

Chapter 8

Sovereignty

From a vibratory standpoint, there is little difference between personal and national sovereignty—the latter being the outer reflection of the former. Sovereignty, as interpreted and experienced in the consciousness of the Grid, is an expression of *divide et impera* under the disguise of a twisted interpretation of freedom. Translated into the language of Oneness consciousness, sovereignty means personal and collective responsibility to act as conscious co-creative entities in sync with the fundamental Laws governing existence.

> *Within the Grid, sovereignty is a concept. With* cor publicum, *sovereignty dissolves in its experience.*

Sovereignty is the structural architecture of the Grid: a society trying to hold balance on a teetering structure: the cropped pyramid. Within the Grid, sovereignty is the dream of power, the dream of freedom, the dream of happiness.

Law is the structural architecture of a society attuned to Heart Wisdom, a society experiencing balance on a grounded structure: *cor publicum*. Law is power, Law is freedom, Law opens the pathway to happiness.

Within the Grid, sovereignty is a concept. With *cor publicum,* sovereignty dissolves in its experience.

Chapter 9

Property

In *cor publicum,* the concept of property is more accurately reflected in the word "boundaries." The importance of boundaries needs careful consideration. Interestingly, from within the Grid, a society that is guided by the wisdom of the Heart, a society that is equally guided by reason and feelings, a society that is guided by Love, is often misunderstood as a permissive, unmanageable society that does not respect individual boundaries.

> *In* cor publicum, *the concept of property is more accurately reflected in the word "boundaries."*

What is the meaning of boundaries? Boundaries are the outer lines of a natural vibrational field around each being that expresses the sacredness of life. As such, boundaries honor the innate freedom and power of each human being, while also being expressions of gentleness, in consideration of human vulnerability. Property is a physical expression of these sacred boundaries, and as such property is sacred.

Within *cor publicum,* the sacredness of boundaries is assumed, and thus honored. Boundaries are a fundamental premise around which the collective organizes. Boundaries are not pulled and pushed in a continuous tug-of-war. Boundaries are revered and through the guidance of Heart Wisdom allowed to find their point of balance in each changing circumstance.

Heart Wisdom will reveal that some boundaries are fixed, while others are malleable. Heart Wisdom always offers the key ingredients to balancing seemingly conflicting boundaries. Heart Wisdom holds the formula capable of honoring the sacredness of boundaries in balance with the whole. When we assume and embody the intrinsic inviolability of boundaries, rather than assuming their violability and precariousness, a relaxation occurs that expands the vibrational field around boundaries. As a result, this field is more efficient in finding the point of balance.

> *Boundaries honor the innate freedom and power of each human being, while also being expressions of gentleness, in consideration of human vulnerability.*

Within *cor publicum,* the presence of internal boundaries is experienced regardless of the outward expression of such boundaries. This experience increases the likelihood that the outward boundaries reflect the spaciousness of internal boundaries. In a society guided by Heart Wisdom and kindness, a relaxation happens that extends boundaries, that

Heart Wisdom not only provides the most effective protection of property, but also increases its size and value.

increases the spaciousness that each individual, collective, and nation experiences. In other words, Heart Wisdom not only provides the most effective protection of property, but also increases its size and value.

When grounded solely in the mind, boundaries are the outer limits of a cage that perpetuates powerlessness. When grounded in the Heart, boundaries are the outer expression of freedom and power.

Chapter 10

Property and Land

What does "ownership" mean? What is the source of property rights? What are community property and personal property? And what is their proper balance within *cor publicum*? Are there any differences between land and personal property?

Land

Land belongs to itself. Land cannot be owned. Ownership presupposes a severing, which is at the core of the many disputes, conflicts, and battles over the centuries. As long as land is deemed to belong to an entity other than itself, the land emanates a discordant vibration. This vibration is mostly dormant and can be detected in subtle yet dramatic ways; sometimes it openly emits a stream of destructive energy into the mass consciousness.

Land has a powerful emanation that human consciousness has misunderstood for the longest time. Land has a raw primal emanation that becomes livable for humans when its energy is filtered through and

> *Land has a raw primal emanation that becomes livable for humans when its energy is filtered through and gently brought into the Heart.*

gently brought into the Heart. There, it has a vibration that is calibrated to resonate with human consciousness. The human Heart is capable of translating the Heart vibration of the land into a livable and sustainable environment, a reciprocal vibratory exchange that sustains flourishing growth.

Within the Grid, land has been deemed a lifeless object to be taken and used at will. Land has been considered a commodity to be owned, negotiated, and transferred. Land has been deemed a primary right, a means to control, a means to separate, a means to exercise power, a means to assert and rigidify identity. Land is the primary source of identity for individuals and nations. It

> *The moment land is released from the claim of ownership, it offers itself.*

is the asset through which we define and experience a sense of self, a sense of security, the senseless meaning of self.

The relationship between land and identity is an ancient one; it is the main theme defining the story of our times. Over thousands of years the claiming of land by humans has had its impact. Often battles over land have been attributed to the rulers and inhabitants of that land. But often these battles originated from the land itself. These battles were captured and misread by those living on the land and mistakenly channeled into the enemy claiming the land.

At the core of this dynamic is a deep misunderstanding of the inherent power of land, of the individuality of land, of the space that land is claiming when approached out of sync. When approached from the premise of separation rather than from the space of Heart Wisdom, land will reflect such a frame of consciousness. As long as land is approached as an identity that can be grabbed, land emanates a vibration that perpetuates the battle to own land. When approached from the premise of Heart co-creation, land seeks to merge with the human collective Heart pulsating in sync with life.

Land is the asset through which we define and experience a sense of self, a sense of security, the senseless meaning of self.

The simple truth is that land cannot be owned as long as it is wanted as a possession: the moment land is released from the claim of ownership, it offers itself. Land makes itself available in sync with its own individual power, with its own collective power, and it emanates a frequency that flows freely in the web of the planet and the human collective to continuously find the intersection of human and planetary needs. As long as land is owned, the frequency flowing from the land is out of sync and incapable of finding the intersection just described.

Who are we as a nation if we do not have land, if we can not claim land? Are we the land? Is the land us?

Land ownership is a charged basic agreement of the social contract of the Grid, because it is so intimately linked with identity. Without land ownership there is a loss of identity. Without individual and collective identity there is no ground to stand on.

The key to a new understanding of land and ownership is reverence. It is a collective act of reverence toward the very "thing" that gives us a sense of identity, even though illusionary. The key to a new understanding of land and ownership is the courage to ask the question who am I? Who are we as a nation if we do not have land, if we can not claim land? Are we the land? Is the land us?

In the segregated realm of Grid, that which makes us vulnerable must be overpowered, claimed, taken, and suppressed.

Land gives us a primal sense of security. Land is the foundation of our bodies in flesh. Land is the womb that holds our physical bodies. Because of the intimate and primal connection between land, our bodies, and our identity, the vulnerability is immense. And in the segregated realm of Grid, that which makes us vulnerable must be overpowered, claimed, taken, and suppressed. The quest for

Land seeks to be freed of claims.

control over the uncontrollable generates the claim of land ownership; it generates a continuous battle over land; it generates collective systems set up to monopolize and then seize land.

Land seeks to be freed of claims. Land seeks to be primal power offering itself to the needs of the people. Land seeks to be freed from the cage of ownership. Land seeks to be felt and interacted with through the wisdom of the Heart. It is Heart Wisdom within individuals, within collectives, that is capable of

Land seeks to be felt and interacted with through the wisdom of the Heart.

weaving a new relationship with the land, thus serving each individual and the whole simultaneously. It is in the vibration of the Heart that the pathway of communication between humans and land can be found. It is through the vibration of the Heart that the primal power of land can be infused into human beings.

It is in the vibration of the Heart that the knowing of belonging, the knowing of being held, the knowing of safety, is strengthened.

Within the old social contract, the pathway of communication with the land has been intentionally severed by the lone ruler (the mind) and relegated into a pagan set of beliefs for the few. The consequence is that the masses keep scrambling for a sense of belonging, of identity, and they keep scrambling for safety in a never-ending unwinnable battle for land.

The untamable, destructive monologues with land are moved into mature exchanges that honor the primal power of land and the primal needs of the collective.

When land is freed from the claim of ownership, from the assumption of severance, and when the communication with individuals, with collectives, with nations is re-established through the language of the Heart, land can engage in a mutually sustainable exchange. Then, a muffled land seeking to explode and a childish collective seeking to stamp on the land in a tantrum for control are both freed into maturity. The untamable, destructive monologues with land are moved into mature exchanges that honor the primal power of land and the primal needs of the collective.

Property Rights

Property rights within *cor publicum* are understandings of how to weave the needs of the individuals and the collective in harmony with the land. Within the new social contract, land is freed from identity, and iden-

> *The grounding stability that comes from property rights in the old social contract is found in the grounding freedom of intentional exchange with the land in the new social contract.*

tity has surrendered its grip on land. The collective has reached the maturity to internalize safety, security, the knowing of belonging, and it finds them within the creative individual and co-creative collective weaving, rather than in the land. Within *cor publicum,* land is not tied in the rigid structure of ownership, but interplays with collective wisdom. Land is included in the weaving of society's needs. The grounding stability that comes from property rights in the old social contract is found in the grounding freedom of intentional exchange with the land in the new social contract.

Balancing Individual and Common Needs

Within *cor publicum,* individual boundaries and choices are honored. When the intentions of the society are articulated and held from within the chambers of the

Heart, right relation with the land emerges. Individual and common needs are integrated, and the delicate balance between them is woven together by the vector of intention of the unfolding collective. Land is, through a collective agreement, assigned and offered to those living in balanced relation. It is the wisdom of a collective aligned with the vibration

Proprietary agreements based within cor publicum *are a three-way exchange of reciprocal understandings.*

of the collective Heart that determines which land is assigned to serve the common good and which land is assigned to each individual.

A collective aligned with Heart Wisdom is one that hears the voice of the land, one that is capable of receiving the primal power of land and transmitting it to its inhabitants in a resonant exchange. Each collective assigns land to individuals in agreements founded in a vibratory exchange between the individual and the land, in a code of reciprocal listening, in codified language that recog-

Within cor publicum, *the distinction between individual and public property remains.*

nizes the vital elements of the exchange. This code is not a rigidly structured set of rules that originates from within the cropped pyramidal structure, but an expression of fundamentally organic principles of sustainable co-existence. This code is an expression of vibratory keys that gives healthy access to the power of land.

The proprietary agreements within the Grid have excluded the voice of the land, making them two-way agreements between the giver and the receiver of land within a set of transactional codes. Proprietary agreements based within *cor publicum* are a three-way exchange of reciprocal understandings within a set of vibratory encodings set to access the balance of the whole through the wisdom of the Heart. They are an exchange woven together by an intentional Heart-based connection between the individual, the collective, and the land.

The nature of assigning and using land is not transactional.

Within *cor publicum,* the distinction between individual and public property remains. However, property is understood as a caretaking agreement. Like the individual, land belongs to itself and cannot be severed. Land, when honored, offers itself to maintain the balance of the whole in all relations. This balance is identifiable by a collective that has agreed to attune itself to the wisdom teachings of the Heart.

The nature of assigning and using land is not transactional. It is an act of listening, an offering to tune into the essence of land, which in turn offers a welcoming home dedicated to nurturing the needs of the receiver. Property rights express the responsibilities of the receiver toward the land, rather than protecting the land owner from intervention by other individuals and the collective.

When the collective agrees that nobody owns land other than the land itself, no individual or collective can make a claim on the land. The agreements between individuals and collectives are thus meant to be a simple understanding of responsibilities toward the

> *Property rights express the responsibilities of the receiver toward the land.*

land, rather than toward each other. The essential agreement is only the one between the individual and the land or, in the case of public property, between the collective and the land. The intimacy of this vertical agreement is what strengthens the individual connection with the land and brings life once again to an exchange that within the Grid has entirely lost its life force, as a result of the severance and the purely horizontal nature of property rights.

This realignment of property rights shifts the explosive power of land—once muffled in its severance from those living on it—into a new vibratory field that balances the resources of land and the needs of the people.

Value of Labor

How can individual or collective labor on land be valued? From the standpoint of Grid consciousness, there is a flawed understanding that within a system governed by the teachings of the Heart, individual needs are curbed. There is an underlying premise that the wisdom of the Heart runs contrary to the sovereignty of the individual. From within the mental construct of the Grid, Heart Wisdom is a dangerous undertaking.

> *There is an underlying premise that the wisdom of the Heart runs contrary to the sovereignty of the individual.*

The essence of the Heart Wisdom teachings is to weave a *modus operandi* in sync with all life, including the one defined as individual labor. The essence of Heart Wisdom is to weave together what to the mind appear as opposing forces: individual property rights and public property rights at the root of labor value.

Heart Wisdom weaves together what appears to be a paradox to the constricted realm of the mind. Heart Wisdom opens the space to harmoniously sync what appears irreconcil-

> *Heart Wisdom opens the space to harmoniously sync what appears irreconcilable.*

able: the needs of individuals are met organically from the plane of consciousness of each individual. No rigid form is imposed to define the content of needs, the framing of needs. The fulfillment of individual needs is a natural result when operating from Heart Wisdom.

Honoring the primal need of individuals to feel safe and secure is a Heart-logical consequence of a society that it is attuned with the balance of the whole. For some, security comes from a house to safely rely on. Some individuals derive their sense of safety and security from a different source. Within *cor publicum,* needs are not rigidly assumed and defined, but

> *Within* cor publicum, *needs are not rigidly assumed and defined, but inquired about and met.*

inquired about and met, when necessary, in a co-creative process that generates a field of loving care, respect, and support for each individual.

When society has collectively agreed that land owns itself, that each individual has a primal need for a safe and nurturing environment, that the meaning of home is organic and continually evolving, then the collective wisdom is geared to generate a powerful field in which land, individuals, and collectives are equally engaged in and equally responsible for creating proprietary forms and agreements that honor the needs of the whole.

Standards of Care

The primary responsibility for the care of land lies in the individual. The individual who lives within the understandings of *cor publicum* is equally and simultaneously attuned to his specific needs, those of the whole, and those of the land.

When individuals who have become adult citizens engage and move from within their Hearts, co-existence is smooth and highly respectful. The individual Heart—when consciously and intentionally linked to the Heart Wisdom of the collective—is already including the needs of the collective in the definition of its own needs. In this sense, *cor publicum* is a mature, self-regulatory society in which the collective is accessed not to curb, direct, and control the individual, but to continuously inform, expand, and strengthen individual wisdom with collective wisdom.

> Cor publicum *is a mature, self-regulatory society in which the collective is accessed to strengthen individual wisdom with collective wisdom.*

Private and Public Property

In *cor publicum,* rights are conceived as space. Thus, the relevant distinction is between private and public space. Both spaces are continuously communicating with each other, because *cor publicum* is a living body that pulsates in an ever-continuing movement to harmonize the whole.

Within *cor publicum,* citizens are the organs of a healthy collective body that with each breath seeks to feed and nurture the whole body, while maintaining the integrity of the space of each organ, of each function.

Within *cor publicum,* private and public are not at odds and battling each other for survival, for more land, as do healthy and sick cells in a cancerous body. In *cor publicum,* the private and public body both cooperate in the awareness that maintaining healthy individual space, maintaining healthy organs and functions, is how the whole collective body can sustainably function. Equally, the private and public body both cooperate in the awareness that maintaining healthy public and shared space is how the individual body can sustainably function. What weaves public and private space together in balance is the pulsation of the Heart, is the knowing and wisdom of the Heart.

> *Within* cor publicum, *resources are held, nurtured, and sustained in the awareness of the whole, rather than separated in the battling wars of the Grid.*

Within *cor publicum,* resources such as water, air, forests, and mountains are naturally public spaces, as they are the blood, the oxygen, and the membranes that are needed to sustain each other individually and collectively. Rather than a political dogmatic statement, this assignment of land is common wisdom that flows from the awareness of Law, the awareness of what sustains life.

Within *cor publicum,* resources are held, nurtured, and sustained in the awareness of the whole, rather than separated in the battling wars of the Grid. Again, where the interaction between the individual and the collective is based on the agreement of co-creation, of infinite possibilities and abundance, resources are approached from a mature and adult frame of reference, rather than from that of a child battling over a precious and rare toy.

Chapter 11

Whole Body of Law

Meaning

The whole body of Law is a body grounded in its whole essence. The whole body of Law is an exploration, not a finished product, not a set of certain and firm rules, which is the very characteristic that has kept Law trapped. The whole body of Law is a continuing, evolving being that is alive and breathing and reinventing itself as new issues arise. It is a radical shift from what we perceive as law within the

The whole body of Law is articulated by a mind at the service of the Heart.

Grid. The whole body of Law is rooted in the wisdom of the Heart and is articulated by a mind at the service of the Heart. It is the voice of the Heart.

There are many perspectives from which the whole body of Law can be illuminated. Fundamental to all perspectives is that the language of the whole body of Law, the language of the Heart vibration, is foreign to the current body of law. It is a cryptic language that the servants of the law will struggle with and dismiss at first. That is the nature of the lone mind: a well-armored set of beliefs that, when threatened, fights back for its own survival ... mostly out of fear.

The current body of law is like a body that was designed to breathe carbon dioxide but somewhere and somehow always intuited that only the qualities of the vibration of oxygen were making it healthy. Now this body is asked to redesign itself and learn to function with oxygen. But the comfort of breathing carbon dioxide, the benefit of maintaining the *status quo*, i.e., the fear of change and insanity when entering a world that is not controlled by the mind, is far less threatening.

> *The language of the whole body of Law is a cryptic language that the servants of the law will struggle with and dismiss at first.*

Again, there are many levels from which the whole body of Law can be approached: from the microscopic plane of existence—i.e., the whole body of Law within the individual; from the macroscopic plane of existence—i.e., the whole body of Law within a community, state, or nation, or between countries; or from the plane of protecting and fostering life—i.e., the whole body of Law within planets, stars, and other celestial systems.

All these planes are intertwined. When one system is changed, all others are impacted in ways that are more visible, transparent, and tangible than when we are operating from the exclusive and segregated realm of the mind. In the vibration of the Heart and in the consciousness of the unknown factor, all these bodies are one. The whole body of Law is the body of Oneness.

Origins

The validity of a law has been construed to originate in the perceived legitimacy of its source—God, the king or monarch, the clergy, or the people, as defined by the current understanding of who *the people* were and are. For the most part, the source of legitimacy and authority has been linked to the vibration of a specific gender—and in the last several thousands years to a male vibration. A perceived legitimate source of law has also been found in nature as conceived at that time.

> *The consciousness entrapped in a cropped law categorizes the source of the whole body of Law as one that needs to be segregated and relegated to the religious-spiritual-pagan compartment.*

The source of the whole body of Law freed from its linear mind entrapment and linked to its own Heart pulsation is found in the cosmic Heart Mind, in the black hole of formlessness, where the seeds of all potential forms reside, waiting to be activated by the act of intention and choice. The source of the whole body of Law is found in the ever-spinning spiral of creation moved and governed by the Laws of existence.

In its incapacity to grasp the complexity of this source, the consciousness entrapped in a cropped law categorizes the source of the whole body of Law, as one that needs to be segregated and relegated to the religious-spiritual-pagan compartment.

From the standpoint of the entrapped consciousness that has created its own definition of legitimacy, acknowledging the source of universal Laws as the source of the whole body of Law is inconceivable and a threat to its own survival. The basic premise of cropped law is that what is not explicable in linear terms does not have legitimacy. This premise is a self-predicament, because the consciousness at the core of cropped law will always deny itself access to its full potential: the vibration of Love and compassion, the wisdom of the Heart.

The freeing of Law happens through a collective choice that recognizes the legitimacy of the Heart Wisdom teachings as a way to organize life between citizens and nations.

The freeing of Law happens through a collective choice that recognizes the legitimacy of the Heart Wisdom teachings as a way to organize life between citizens and nations. The freeing of Law happens through a collective choice that takes these teachings out of the religious/spiritual/pagan compartment. Once the collective choice is made to grant the vibration of Love the legitimacy to be a concrete process to bring Law to its full potential, 100% of the source becomes available. At this point, the potential for generating a world society that governs itself in a just and sustainable manner is much higher.

The source of the whole body of Law resides in the ever-changing whole—the realm of the illuminated mind, the realm of the Heart, the realm of the known, the realm of the unknown, the realm of the explicable and the realm of the inexplicable—all governed by the universal Laws of existence.

Chapter 12

Fundamental Freedoms

Meaning

In our plane of consciousness, we often talk about fundamental freedoms as if they were a given concept inherent in a democracy, as if they were available only to certain people, in certain countries, and under certain circumstances.

Freedom is an undeletable and untouchable sphere of influence that is inherent in consciousness. It is a vibrational key that unlocks the creation process. It is a vibration whose frequency is accessible to different degrees, depending on the level of consciousness.

> *Freedom is an undeletable and untouchable sphere of influence that is inherent in consciousness.*

At its core, freedom is the space in between. It is the empty space in a civilization. Where emptiness has become an enemy, little freedom is experienced. When emptiness is once again allowed and embraced, freedom can be lived in tangible ways. Emptiness is found in the unknown factor. The unknown factor is accessed through the unlocking of the Grid.

A collective trapped in the Grid approaches freedom mentally and mechanistically. Rather than emptiness, freedom becomes an empty exercise, an exercise of the mind, with little reverberation in the collective.

At its core, freedom is the space in between. It is the empty space in a civilization. Where emptiness has become an enemy, little freedom is experienced.

The sometimes obvious and sometimes subtle collective enslavement can be ended by reclaiming emptiness, by reclaiming space. It is in the emptiness, in the space, that freedom can be found. Freedom begins at the level of the self and then ripples into the collective. This understanding of freedom needs to be taught. When enough people hold this new understanding, the vibrational shift brings about a lifting of the veil of enslavement.

For a very long time, human consciousness has operated from the premise of being "subject of" and caged. Human consciousness has been in a long, continuous fight for freedom, in a continuous striving for more freedom. This attitude presupposes that freedom can be taken away: This is the fundamental flaw in how freedoms are experienced in our level of consciousness.

Moreover, the prevailing program and social contract is to keep filling our cups—with information, with propaganda, with objects, with beliefs. The Grid is programmed to keep filling us and never allow emptiness, because of the dangers inherent in emptiness. This is the most efficient way to perpetuate enslavement, because true freedom can only be unlocked in the emptiness. What ends our collective enslavement is the reclaiming of inner freedom and inner emptiness. When we once again befriend emptiness, individually and collectively, we restore the natural cycle of the ebb and the flow, the natural cycle of filling of the cup followed by emptying the cup. When we choose to embrace this cycle, we create a new social contract: Law and governance emerges; systems emerge based on the fundamental premise that freedom Is and cannot be taken away.

Freeing Freedom

It is fundamental that as citizens we train ourselves to access the various frequency bands of freedom. Some citizens will access a smaller band, others a wider one, but when the premise is the same for everybody, the various bands of consciousness can find and strengthen each other more swiftly and create a new social contract: a new *cor publicum*.

Freedom is at the core of *cor publicum*. And, the legal system that emerges from *cor publicum* is one that is grounded in the unknown factor, the manifestation of emptiness.

Any given regulation or rule is in sync with the vibration of freedom only if allowed to be adapted to the unknown circumstances, to the ever-changing circumstances, to the emptiness of possibilities. These possibilities can be translated into specific choices that resonate with the parties through the wisdom of the Heart, through the guidance of the Heart. It is the Heart Brain that translates emptiness into a practical choice. It is the Heart Brain that translates fullness into a practical choice. It is the Heart Brain that blends fullness and emptiness into wholeness, into Law. It is Law that births *cor publicum*.

> *It is the Heart Brain that blends fullness and emptiness into wholeness, into Law. It is Law that births* cor publicum.

Process

Freedom is now seeking to expand. Other fundamental values such as justice, order, and equality have been energetically trapped within a cropped law and are now seeking to be freed into the vibrant sacred geometry of an ever-changing universe.

We can support this freeing process first through our awareness of the operating system of the Grid and second through the opening of the energetic pathways where the values underlying Law are currently trapped. Most important, we can support this freeing process through a new collective choice grounded in the self, through new conscious collective agreements. These agreements are freeing the genetic codes of Law.

We are embarking upon a revolution of consciousness and an evolution as a species. The unknown factor that is being awakened with the opening of these new pathways is creating temporary confusion and overwhelm. In this time, it is important to nurture the container of change with compassion for humanity as a whole and to hold the vision of eternal life for humanity.

Chapter 13

Whole Body of Governance

The Beginning

The whole body of governance is a whole, grounded form of governance anchored in Law. It is alive. It is created by accessing the Heart—the individual Heart and the collective Heart.

The whole body of governance starts with an inquiry of the citizen into the silence and awareness of his own Heart. It continues with a conscious inquiry and exploration of *cor publicum,* the collective Heart, which is brought to life by the vibrational accumulation of individual citizens practicing the Heart Wisdom teachings in their private *and* public awareness.

The whole body of governance is brought to life when each citizen dwells in the awareness of her own individual Heart, but simultaneously and consciously dwells in the awareness of the collective Heart.

Identifying Cor Publicum

Cor publicum—currently a forgotten life form—is molded into life by the recognition that it exists and that it provides the life force, the inspiration, the strength, the courage, the kindness, the wisdom of the collective to organize itself in a way that maximizes health, well-being, and peace for each individual, as each one chooses.

Cor publicum is to a high degree brought to life by the compassionate practice of the individual alone, as the Heart Wisdom of each individual already integrates the considerations of the collective. Although many individuals practice the wisdom teachings of the Heart, those practices are still not bringing to life *cor publicum,* because they are severed from the collective Heart. Co-creative power and Law are only scantily applied within the private lives of individuals in their collective awareness and almost never within the collectives. The realization of *cor publicum* as a central pulsating source of collective life and its impact on governance is therefore the first step.

> *Although many individuals practice the wisdom teachings of the Heart, those practices are still not bringing to life* cor publicum, *because they are severed from the collective Heart.*

Cor publicum can be identified through the language of the Heart, through acceptance and compassion for the shortcomings of the collective, through Love of the collective for its potential and ability to creatively express itself in alignment with Law.

Cor publicum can be articulated in a statement of creative intention that each collective generates. The voice of *cor publicum* is a language of essence that is accessed in the silence. Silence is therefore an essential collective practice—a far cry from the

> *The voice of* cor publicum *is a language of essence that is accessed in the silence.*

intermittent noise within the Grid. Silence of the Heart is an essential collective skill to be taught early on as a fundamental aspect of civic and public education.

The collective statement of creative intention that emerges from a reading or perception of *cor publicum* is the vector that flows from the foundation—the collective practice, the circle—into the pyramid of the governance form. The statement is regularly re-articulated, as consciousness, when aligned with Law, continually evolves. This continuous adaptation is what keeps *cor publicum* pulsating. It is what keeps the pyramid and the circle continually evolving into new forms.

The collective statement is crafted by groups of citizens from each small community, village, city, region, and nation, and from international collectives. In a holographic manner, statements of each community contain the statements of each international collective, and each statement of international collectives contains the statements of the communities. When operating within the new social contract, the struggles to consolidate so many statements—as often perceived within the cropped pyramidal paradigm—fall away. The content of *cor publicum* is stunningly similar from the community level up to the international level, because it is woven together by Heart vibration, a universal language.

The collective statement of creative intention emerges from a reading or perception of cor publicum.

The content of cor publicum *is stunningly similar from the community level up to the international level, because it is woven together by Heart vibration.*

In the process of drafting the statements of *cor publicum,* each individual and each collective intentionally links to one another. Individuals and collectives are linking the threads of all *cor publicum* statements, from the individual body to the international body, in an intentional conscious act. This act is an expression of public awareness within the individual and an expression of individual awareness within the collective.

This process is the new *modus operandi,* founded in the vibrational awareness of interconnectedness, which allows for a co-creative expression that strengthens *cor publicum* at all levels. The communication among all holographic levels of the individual and the collective to create and operate within *cor publicum* is an exponentially upgraded form of radio, satellite, wireless, and Internet communication. It is based on the most sophisticated computer ever—the whole brain within each being—which is accessed through the Heart Brain. When Heart Wisdom is accessed, the brain is vastly expanded in its potential and has capabilities well beyond the technological achievements within the Grid.

Communication within the new social contract infuses the technological achievements with Heart consciousness, creating an exponential leap in the quality and quantity of data being transmitted.

It is important that each community that articulates the statements expressing *cor publicum* is holographically composed, and that it represents a wide variety of angles, curves, and shapes of society. It is in the geometrical and alchemical diversity of the collective that the hologram is most effective and encompasses the many Heart chambers of *cor publicum.*

Diversity

Diversity is a charged word that has lost significance. Diversity of what? Diversity is intrinsic to life and human nature and thus when used to categorize, it becomes a random act of judgment, a random attempt to control and shape what is not shapeable: the complexity of each human being, each citizen, each pulsating life form. Diversity is ever existent, continually present. Diversity refers to a wide variety of lenses used to analyze a set of circumstances.

Within the new social contract, diversity is an indication that the collective is alive: diversity is seen, recognized, lived, and practiced in every sector and every aspect of collective and individual life. When diversity becomes a claim, a right, a defense, it is an indication that we are dealing with a society that is dying a slow death. Diversity exists in every regard. Diversity exists within a single human being, and the categorizing game of diversity—political, ethnic, national, cultural, religious, gender-based, etc.—is a sign of impotency in the face of the complexity of life.

> *Diversity refers to a wide variety of lenses used to analyze a set of circumstances.*

Political parties and ethnic, national, cultural, and religious groups, for example, which gather for the primary purpose of sharing their assumed and illusionary similarity, are forms created by a desperate mind attempting to bring order to complexity and to control what cannot be caged. Through this categorization, they attempt to create an illusionary sense of safety and protection.

The spontaneous movement of complexity, of diversity, of the pulsating innate lens given to each individual and collective is safe, because it is alive and as such adaptable to the changing circumstances. It is the rigid, unmovable, and thus unnatural structure that is highly vulnerable to breakage; this is a simple principle of physics.

> *The categorizing game of diversity is a sign of impotency in the face of the complexity of life.*

The underlying assumption of political, ethnic, national, cultural or religious groups and the like is that the creativity and diversity of each individual is not only not encouraged, but often—overtly or subtly—rejected ... and homogenization is forced. It is this unmovable and rigid structure of the very concept of political, religious, cultural, or ethnic groups or parties that makes such forms vulnerable. This party or group entrapment keeps most collectives engaged in a never-ending effort to reassert themselves, to survive, in a never-ending war that suppresses diversity as a core principle.

Within the new social contract, diversity is natural and a statement of the obvious. Within the new social contract, the intention is focused on the co-creative process in the awareness of the many ingredients—expressed by diversity—needed to make whole forms more sustainable.

Within the old social contract, groups that share intentions, goals, and affinities are described as "like-minded"—an expression of the mind-focused frame of reference. Within the new social contract, the same is described as a resonance that pierces the walls of the mind to find affinity in the Heart.

Within *cor publicum*—among the many groups created in the awareness of the underlying diversity—resonance is sought to weave together specific groups around a collective intention. Resonance is sought to create the harmonic notes of the collective. Within *cor publicum,* individuals and groups focus

Within the new social contract, diversity is natural and a statement of the obvious.

on resonance that listens and strives to fine-tune the harmonics of the whole, while granting a wide range of possibility in the quest for resonance. Within the Grid, the threads of frozen mind-sets—which often spawn coalitions—are forced into a dissonant chord that ripples into the whole.

Cor publicum recognizes all forms of diversity. It recognizes the diversity of the explosive nature of existence. It recognizes that diversity is the holographic ingredient of source that aims at generating harmonic fields of resonance.

> *Diversity is a resonance that pierces the walls of the mind to find affinity in the Heart.*

For each group, it is thus important to start with an awareness-raising inquiry of the diversity within each individual and collective and to start to mix and blend the holographic ingredients given by each individual and group. When this process is done consciously from within the Heart Brain, a resonant form emerges. When this process is done from within a Heart-disconnected mind, what emerges is a struggle, a steep and dreary road, an insurmountable, dissonant, and hopeless dead end.

Cor publicum is a society that has learned to harness the harmonic tone of joy from the given premise of the diversity of existence. The Grid society is struggling in a self-fabricated hell, in the endless suffering of battling dogmas.

"Form" of Cor Publicum

Cor publicum is always the beginning point. It is the center, the starting point that sets into motion forms of governance—not one form but many forms.

It is important to understand that unlike *res publica,* which was fixed in its form and structure, *cor publicum* is the central core that seeks the governing form most suitable to each collective. *Cor publicum* is founded in the circle, in the wisdom of the people, in the Earth, in the formlessness of the Heart of each human being, in the unknown factor, in the unlimited potential of forms.

Emerging from this foundation is a pyramidal structure that is exclusively composed by the vector of collective intention. The alchemy between the circle and the pyramid blended together by the statement of *cor publicum* brings about a spin that is capable of pulling up from formlessness the form most conducive

> Cor publicum
> *is always the*
> *beginning point.*

to the thriving of each given community, village, city, region, nation ... all the way to the international collective. It is a malleable and pulsating form informed by *cor publicum.*

Cor publicum only starts from a pyramidal structure grounded in the circle. The combination of the circle and the pyramid is what activates the engine of co-creation within *cor publicum,* birthing many forms of governance. Thus, at its core, all forms are self-governing. The forms of *cor publicum* are gestated and birthed within each collective by their own statements and thus keenly in touch with the local circumstances and the needs of each collective, while being woven into the whole.

Within *cor publicum,* there is no tension between sovereignty and the whole, between the sovereignty of individuals and their nations, between the sovereignty of nations and the international collective body. Within *cor publicum,* individual and national sovereignty are fully honored in sync with the circumstances of the whole, because the thread linking these various bodies is defined by the universal vibration of Heart Wisdom. And, Heart Wisdom is capable of embracing the paradox and integrating complexity.

Within *cor publicum,* each community composed of 12, 44, 66, 88, 120, 444, 666, 888, 1200, 4444, 6666 people, and so forth, articulates its core statements and its objectives. These numbers are a sequence that opens a new code of understanding of the collective co-creative process. This sequence is important

The combination of the circle and the pyramid is what activates the engine of co-creation within cor publicum, *birthing many forms of governance.*

in that it sets in motion the weaving of Heart Wisdom. It is through this sequence that the synchronization process of the statements of each community occurs.

The statements may or may not be different when created in a group of 12 versus a group of 44, or 66, or 88, and so forth. It is the Heart-synchronization of these statements that occurs more effectively when membership in each group or community reaches the numbers in the aforementioned sequence.

This sequence represents not rigid numbers but a point of reference that directs the vector of intention of each group or community. The key is that each collective intends to organize itself in such a way that it reaches any chosen number of the sequence. Whether the group or community actually reaches that specific number is of secondary importance. In other words, it is the intention to reach the sequence alone that is fundamental, not the actual number of participants in each group. This is so because the framing of the intention (to reach the sequence) brings about the exact number of participants that allows the group or community to align with Heart Wisdom. In turn, such groups or communities generate statements that can be synchronized with Heart Wisdom.

These numbers are a sequence that opens a new code of understanding of the collective co-creative process.

Each group or community then creates its own governing body to implement the objectives. Some will draw on a legislative, executive, and judiciary body which soon enough, when infused with Heart consciousness, will move from a governing body to a self-governing body. Others will draw on traditional forms of governance, while still others will embrace emergent self-governing forms. All these forms will be continuously brought forth by Heart intelligence, rather than from within the Grid.

Chapter 14

Legislative Body in *Cor Publicum?*

The legislative as conceived in *res publica* is the body that develops statutes and laws. These laws mostly generate from the premises of the Grid. *Cor publicum* holds Law within its essence. It is an expression of Law. It integrates Law.

The question arises whether the current functions of the legislative body are a necessary part of governance. Yes and no. Within *cor publicum,* the legislative body and its functions are re-created, and those re-created functions are a necessary part of governance.

Within the Grid, the legislative body draws its power from its legitimacy. It is concerned about the legitimacy of the source that can impose restrictions of personal freedom and mandate specific behaviors and consequences. In *cor publicum,* the legislative body—as an aspect of the collective body—holds the essence of Law; it operates and pulsates from Law through the co-creative process. The legislative body identifies the situation that it is to focus on and articulates the available choices emerging from Heart Wisdom. The choices are organic and flexibly suitable to the situation, rather than fixed, rigid solutions to a narrowly defined problem.

Within *cor publicum,* each level of the collective—community, neighborhood, village, city, state, nation, inter-nations—creates its own co-creative body for the situation that it faces.

> *In* cor publicum, *the legislative body holds the essence of Law.*

All levels are linked with each other through the shared attunement to Heart Wisdom, to the vibrational Heart core of the collective. To the linear cropped mind, this appears an impossible process, because the mind has clear limits on its ability to process complexity. To the Heart Mind, this creative weaving of the co-creative bodies at each level is the process used to liberate wisdom and to find simple balance in the intricate and complex webbing of society.

> *This creative weaving of the co-creative bodies at each level is the process used to liberate wisdom.*

Many of the situations approached by the collective at each level will be interdependent. For example, a neighborhood situation may have national or even international implications. So the question arises how to coordinate the answers of the co-creative bodies so they actually function. Again, this is a question about the how: once the leap into the unknown is taken, once the core agreements are embodied and Heart Wisdom is thus accessed, the effect of synchronization and balancing of seemingly disconnected and insurmountable issues will be stunning to the mind and logical to the Heart.

> *In* cor publicum *the effect of synchronization and balancing of seemingly disconnected and insurmountable issues will be stunning to the mind and logical to the Heart.*

When each collective body —from the neighborhood to the international level —holds within its co-creative process both the awareness of the multidimensional nature of the situation and the intention to generate choices reflective of the multilayered essence of the situation, then the resulting choices are in resonance with the whole.

Within *cor publicum,* the legislative body is a co-creative wisdom-articulating body whose legitimacy is grounded in the teachings of the Heart. It is a body grounded in the integrity of the process, grounded in loving-kindness, compassion, courage, respect, freedom, and responsibility. It is grounded in a healthy individual and collective self-esteem and, most important, in humility. It is grounded in the humble realization that we are continuously learning from evolving Heart Wisdom.

With *cor publicum,* the functions of the co-creative bodies are similar to the ones in *res publica,* in that the participants engage in an exchange of ideas and possibilities. In *res publica,* participants are representatives; in *cor publicum,* each citizen exclusively represents himself. The delegation of power inherent in representatives creates a

> *In* res publica, *participants are representatives; in* cor publicum, *each* citizen exclusively *represents himself.*

segregation of power, which in turn stifles the process, restricts the pathway into the pool of wisdom, and thwarts the very essence of *cor publicum.*

Where power is freed and channeled through the voice of each co-creative citizen, of each silent citizen, where power is freed through the co-creative process, the essence of Law is expressed.

It is through the wisdom of the circle that Law is activated to reach into the pyramid and spin beyond its limits and then to offer—in a downward-grounding spiral—new choices to situations, new forms, even new processes of self-governance. All that is brought about in this way is grounded in the pulsating wisdom of the Heart of a whole collective body.

Chapter 15

Executive Body in *Cor Publicum?*

Who is in charge of ensuring that the choices created are implemented? And what about situations that require a quick collective answer? Within *cor publicum,* the "executive" aspect is vibrationally linked to the original meaning of the associated verb, "execute": to carry into effect. Choices generated in the co-creative process are held with care in the transitional phase between the identification process and the practical implementation of the chosen possibility.

This transition is a delicate in-between phase, a void, and as such in *res publica* often prone to misuse. It is often in this phase that the webbing and thread of legislative intention falls off the field generated by the legislative body. Often this essential vibrational link is severed in this void, and the original source and intention is suffocated by the many interventions and the battling occurring in this phase.

The fragility and precariousness of this in-between phase is unconsciously and at times consciously well understood and exploited, often to further vested interests and to divert legislative intention into the hands of battling minds.

In *res publica,* lawyers trained within the cropped pyramidal frame of consciousness are given sophisticated tools for using the void to divert legislative intention and engage in the battle of minds. In this void, lawyers generate new laws tailored to the needed outcome. Within *res publica*—because of the mere unconscious awareness of the risks inherent in this transition—the executive body is set to generate a shadow legislative body.

> *Within* res publica *the executive body is set to generate a shadow legislative body.*

Within *cor publicum,* this void, this transition, is consciously held, and the intentions and choices generated in the co-creative process are carefully carried into implementation. The in-between phase is consciously bridged by the vibrational thread of integrity. The void is held and infused with Heart Wisdom. The choices are carried into effect over the

> *Within* cor publicum *the choices are carried into effect over the bridge of the void, by delicate servants attuned to the integrity and power inherent in Law.*

bridge of the void, by delicate servants attuned to the integrity and power inherent in Law.

Within *cor publicum*—as within the legislative body— the functions of the executive body organically emerge from the co-creative process. The executive body is not a segregated public body, but a body that is held within each co-creative citizen. Within *cor publi-cum,* legislative, executive, and judiciary bodies are not separate entities. The co-creative (legislative), implementing (executive), and balancing (judiciary) functions in *res publica* are

> *Each individual and each collective is holding space for the co-creative, implementing, and balancing functions of the public body of* cor publicum.

held in *cor publicum* at different levels: fundamentally by each individual, because each individual awakens to her personal and collective responsibility to create the form of governance she is living in; and fundamentally by each collective that has awakened in this way. Each individual and each collective both—even if not actively engaged—vibrationally infuses the web of society with Heart Wisdom. All are holding space for the co-creative, implementing, and balancing functions of the public body of *cor publicum.*

Furthermore, it is the co-creative process that individuates the servants of each implementation: those willing to and capable of embracing the responsibility of implementation with integrity are individuated as intuited and guided by the collective Heart. Those capable of bridging the void through their dedication to the whole, and their individual and collective wisdom, are individuated by a collective body freed

> *It is the co-creative process that individuates the servants of each implementation.*

into the whole Heart Brain. In other words, those capable of understanding the language of words, of sounds, of images, of the multifaceted language of the Heart are the servants of implementation.

Within *cor publicum,* the executive functions are interwoven in the web of society. Individuals, collectives, and servants of implementation equally share in the responsibility to carry into effect the intentions and choices generated through the organic process of the pulsating public Heart.

Chapter 16

Judiciary in *Cor Publicum?*

Meaning

For a long time, justice has been perceived as a transactional act. It has been perceived as an act of giving and receiving—from one person to another—to redeem a wrongful act and to rebalance in the spirit of equitable distribution. Justice has been conceived and practiced as a three-way road between a judge or jury, a person or entity that has been wronged or damaged, and a person or entity that has a claim. Justice creates a triangular field, a pyramidal vertical structure.

We now consider an expanded vibration of justice and move beyond its mostly transactional nature. Yes, many treatises about justice have been written, inspired by the spirit of this untouchable energy. And yet the execution of justice has become for the most part a transactional exchange. True justice generates from within the spiral of Love. It generates from within the compassionate Heart, the sacred chambers of the Heart.

Justice is a vibration. Justice is the glue that weaves together the stories of people through the gate of the Heart. It is the work of the true servant of justice to hold the space of the sacred Heart and listen to the words of wisdom flowing from this space.

The execution of justice has become for the most part a transactional exchange. True justice generates from within the spiral of Love.

Justice is the common thread that reconnects people at the vibrational level of the Heart. It links the Hearts of individuals and collectives. Each weaving of justice contributes to the wider web of justice and allows the planet to maintain balance. The web of justice connects with the Oneness consciousness matrix which in turn nurtures and strengthens the web of justice. It is a vibratory exchange that serves the whole.

For a long time, justice has been a slippery dream that escapes most courts, even in the case of the many well-intentioned efforts to serve justice. The vibrational quality of justice is hooked into the Grid, and therefore its vibrational essence finds only limited expression. This explains why the collective feels that justice does not exist on this place of reality, or if so, that it resides in the "separate" realms of religion, spirituality, or paganism.

Justice within *cor publicum* is redefined. Justice is a pathway of Love, compassion, and forgiveness. These vibrational signatures originate in the Heart chambers and flow through and between the matrix of individuals, organizations, communities, and nations, creating a vibrational web around the globe that naturally seeks to merge with Oneness consciousness.

Servants of Justice

How is justice served within the judiciary body of *cor publicum*? Within *cor publicum,* the Judge becomes the servant of justice. She is an individual of high integrity, as determined by her dedication to the teachings of the Heart. The long-standing emphasis on the mental, linear qualities of the Judge is a result of the Grid consciousness. Such consciousness allows little room for anything other than its own vibration. As the Grid is weakened, unlocked, and eventually disintegrated, the servant of justice is selected for both his linear expertise

The servant of justice is capable of holding the vibrational space of Oneness—the source of justice.

and his integrity in living according to Heart Wisdom. The servant of justice is capable of holding the vibrational space of Oneness—the source of justice.

The position of the servant of justice shifts from being at the top of the pyramidal structure to being in the circle, along with the parties that seek justice. This shift in position allows the servant of justice to connect vibrationally with the web of Oneness consciousness and to tap into the unknown factor. This factor needs to be included to allow for the vibration of the dispute to rise to the vibration of justice and balance.

When the servant of justice operates from within the geometry of the circle, an alchemical marriage between the creative forces contained in the circle is set into motion. This process generates a vibrational spin, which in turn creates a pyramid that is grounded in the Heart. From this alchemical space of creation, whole forms emerge, and the potential for true justice arises.

The position of the servant of justice shifts from being at the top of the pyramidal structure to being in the circle, along with the parties that seek justice.

To move from potential to experience, the act of intention and choice is needed. And in this regard, justice is an act of choice and intention, mostly by the parties in a dispute, but also by the servant of justice. Her role is to create a vibrational field where the potential for lived justice is exponentially increased, to create a vibrational environment conducive to a choice that aligns with justice. Further, she seeks to create an alignment with the web of Oneness consciousness that inspires the parties to reconnect to justice.

For several thousand years, the justice system has been conceived and practiced on the premise that justice is given from an external source: from an entity external to the parties, such as a court or a judge. The judiciary system is based on a process that assigns to a third "neutral" entity the task of finding justice.

This delegation of power is a core aspect of the old social contract and as such is incapable of bringing forth justice. Even many of the emerging forms of alternative dispute resolution—although closer to a vibration conducive to justice—are not bringing forth justice, because they are generated from within the Grid, from within the artificial cropped pyramid.

> *For several thousand years, the justice system has been conceived and practiced on the premise that justice is given from an external source.*

Again, to open the gate to the vibration of justice, we need first to recognize the collective agreements contained in the Grid. A new social contract founded in the heartland unlocks the Grid. This process frees the vibration of justice and propels justice back into the hands of the parties in dispute, deepening the realization that justice is waiting for our hands to sculpt it into a whole form. While holding the vibration of justice, the role of the servant of justice is to assist in the sculpting and to provide ingredients and tools that perfect the form of the new flexible sculpture.

Criminal Justice

Serving criminal justice is slightly more complex, and yet the same basic principles apply. When the justice system is infused with this new understanding of justice and is activated by the intention of its servants to hold space in this new way, criminal justice is beneficially influenced. It is a leg in a healthy Heart-centered body that breathes oxygen, rather than a leg in a partially functioning body disconnected from its life force that breathes carbon dioxide.

Servants of Criminal Justice

When harm and violence are involved, the role of the servant of justice is to create space around the offender and the harmed party. This space-creating function is different than the vibration of punishment, which ultimately cages both sides.

The role of the servant of criminal justice is to hold the space of the Heart and channel the vibration of unconditional compassion and forgiveness, the core ingredients of justice. This role is a far cry from the traditional role of criminal judges, which focuses on mechanistic statutory analysis of a behavior. It is also different than the role held for thousands of years by the clergy and other religious figures, where forgiveness was traded for a specific set of beliefs or behaviors, according to specific values and was consistently misused as a means of control.

> *This space-creating function is different than the vibration of punishment, which ultimately cages both sides.*

The role of the true servant of criminal justice is unconditional in its essence. The servant of criminal justice creates the additional spaciousness required in the weaving of unconditional compassion and forgiveness when the circumstances are painful. The servant of justice contributes to the freeing of the offender from her own Grid of unconsciousness. The spaciousness created by the servant of justice momentarily frees the harmed party from the pressure of forced forgiveness. The role of the servant of justice in creating spaciousness reflects his awareness that in the wake of a violent act the weaving of the thread of justice is more precarious and requires a skillful balancing act. It is like sculpting a whole form

> *The role of the true servant of criminal justice is unconditional in its essence.*

on an unstable foundation. This role requires patience and care and deep trust in the unknown factor to guide the process by which justice will emerge.

Process

The difference between creating spaciousness and punishing rests in the integrity of the intention. Becoming a servant of justice is a tall order and requires a deep dedication to the wisdom teachings of the Heart.

After a criminal act is committed, the offender is held in custody. The offender is held with the intention of "custody" in its original meaning—"care and protection." Similarly, the community is activated and asked to hold custody and space for the harmed party. The servant of criminal justice assesses whether space is needed between the parties and,

As long as the wisdom teachings of the Heart are severed from the criminal process, the vibration of justice cannot be woven into the matrix of society.

in sync with the unknown factor, allows the right timing of their coming together to emerge from the parties themselves.

The role of the servant of criminal justice is to recognize and articulate what is emerging. Once the right timing has emerged, the parties come together to express their pain and understandings. After having heard each other's stories, they are each asked to put themselves in the shoes of the other. The servant of criminal justice observes whether an acknowledgment of the inflicted pain is possible and whether there is room for forgiveness. This process can take much time and requires much patience, as forgiveness is a layered process.

The role of the servant of criminal justice is to be present as a conduit for justice and to facilitate and support the healing process through which justice can be served. As long as the wisdom teachings of the Heart are severed from the criminal process, the vibration of justice—which is intimately connected to compassion and forgiveness—cannot be woven into the matrix of society.

Integrity of the Servant of Justice

The question arises how to define whether a servant of justice is capable of holding the space of Oneness, compassion, and forgiveness and how to prevent the abuses so well documented in history.

This justice system is a natural consequence of the shift in collective consciousness.

The framing of this question implies a different order of manifestation. This justice system is a natural consequence of the shift in collective consciousness. The vibrational environment has changed considerably and the level of collective consciousness has risen. This shift has been gradual, and bits and pieces of this new justice system are already emerging and taking hold.

However, as long as the Grid is in place, and until a new collective conscious choice is made, the seeds of this new justice system struggle to survive. These seeds live in a hostile environment, like healthy new cells trying to survive in a cancerous body. As the new seeds are watered and the Grid is unlocked, the above question becomes moot. At that point, access to Oneness consciousness is natural and more visible, and whether a servant of justice is in alignment with the wisdom teachings of the Heart is easy to determine.

Chapter 17

Nations and Countries within *Cor Publicum*

Cor publicum recognizes boundaries at various levels: individual boundaries, boundaries of specific collectives, and potentially the boundaries of nations or countries.

Nations and countries are proclaimed on the premise of protection, on the premise of a fear of invasion, on the premise of potential loss of self-determination.

Nations and countries within the Grid are born in an act of contraction, at times masked as an act of expansion. Within *cor publicum,* collectives are born out of the awareness of expansiveness, the awareness of spaciousness and the sacredness of boundaries. Within *cor publicum,* the collectives are at their conception infused with the awareness of the sacredness and inviolability of their inner essence, because they are born from Heart Wisdom. Such collectives trust the variability inherent in life.

Within the Grid, nations and countries are born as collectives that wrap around the vector of a story—called "his-story." This story is often based on certain events placed in context by a cropped pyramidal mind. The mind inflates and deflates events, idealizing or demonizing them in its familiar dualistic and adversarial pattern. Nations and countries are often sustained by stories of martyrs that the "other" deems heroes, and stories of heroes that the "other" deems martyrs. These stories are often ungrounded and illusionary tales of a perceived reality.

> *Nations and countries within the Grid are born in an act of contraction, at times masked as an act of expansion. Within* cor publicum, *collectives are born out of the awareness of spaciousness.*

Collectives within the Grid create nations and countries, in that they gather around stories of pain and suffering. Collectives within *cor publicum* gather around their awareness of Heart Wisdom.

Collectives within the Grid vibrationally perpetuate the events around which they originally gathered. These collectives trap themselves in a never-ending cycle of suffering. They lock their own nations and countries into cages, into fortresses, continually concerned with their own safety, continually on alert, continually waiting to be attacked, continually losing their life force in perennial fight-or-flight mode.

Eighty-six percent of the countries on the planet are fully embedded in their contracted histories, and the remaining 14% are partially embedded.

Within cor publicum, collectives gather around intentions rather than events and stories.

At times, events that generated nations and countries were so traumatic that they understandably motivated collective actions. However, many collectives are unaware of the debilitating impact of the poor quality of the seeds that spawned their nations. It is not the past events themselves that create the debilitation, but the unconscious perpetuation of the events through the reinforcement of the his-story of heroism and martyrdom. It is the reinforcement of the pain and suffering that the collective seeks to redeem, and the lack of collective forgiveness, that create the debilitation.

Within cor publicum, collectives are freed from their fight for freedom.

Within *cor publicum,* collectives gather around intentions rather than events and stories; they gather around the intention to be attuned to Heart Wisdom, opening the gate to forms of governance that are expressions of Law; they gather around the intention to cultivate Heart Wisdom as the progenitor of healthy seeds of conception—seeds that conceive healthy and sustainable governance.

Within *cor publicum,* painful events are transformed and embraced with Heart Wisdom; painful events are surrendered, thus freeing the collectives. Within *cor publicum,* collectives are freed from their fight for freedom, and capable of experiencing true freedom rather than chasing the dream of freedom.

Within *cor publicum,* collectives of nations and countries purge their own debilitating DNA, surrender their histories filled with fear, struggle, and pain, and have the courage to choose again. They choose the intention they are gathering around, and they connect to Heart Wisdom to organize their collective actions.

Grid-based nations and countries become different entities within cor publicum.

Through this process, Grid-based nations and countries become different entities within *cor publicum.* They become different forms with respect to their seeds of conception, their vibrational qualities, and their characteristics and purposes.

Beyond Nations and Countries in Cor Publicum

Again, it is important to let go of preconceived forms of collective bodies, such as nations, nation-states, countries, and international organizations. All these forms have been generated from within the cropped pyramidal frame of reference. *Cor publicum* does not assume a specific set of forms: it allows for many organic forms to emerge from the collective Heart, at any scale.

The collective mind is capable of releasing only a limited range of forms. Such forms are fairly rigid and inflexible. Because of the ever-changing nature of circumstances, they lose their effectiveness and are incapable of assimilating the complex and organic interplay of human engagement. These rigid forms are always

> Cor publicum *allows for many organic forms to emerge from the collective Heart, at any scale.*

trying to catch up and force themselves, with great effort and little efficacy, to adapt to changing circumstances. They are like outdated structures that are trying to remain standing although they have long become inadequate to the changing needs of those they serve.

The collective Heart is capable of delivering a wide range of forms in touch with the changing needs and circumstances of the collective, regardless of the size of the collective. Such forms are infused with life force and thus stable in their malleability.

Collective forms within the Grid are like old, unmovable precarious buildings. Collective forms within *cor publicum* are like buildings that are stable and grounded, because they have range of motion built into their structures.

Sovereignty of Collectives?

Sovereignty as understood within the Grid implies contraction, protection, defense from an "other," and it is tightly linked to security. Within *cor publicum*, sovereignty is assumed and inherent in each individual and each organizing collective. Sovereignty is the respect for boundaries, at any scale.

> *Sovereignty within the Grid is a state of dormant and continuous war, waged with impunity.*

Sovereignty within the Grid is a state of dormant and continuous war, waged with impunity. Security is perennially fought for. Sovereignty within *cor publicum* is a direct result of public engagement attuned with Heart Wisdom. Security is created and strengthened with each act of engagement.

When collectives organize and create around the fundamental vibrational essence of Heart Wisdom, the resulting worldwide vibrational field greatly diminishes the likelihood of boundary violations. When such violations occur, no field exists for these violating acts to attach themselves to. Within *cor publicum*, security lies in the integrity of the collective agreement and in the knowing of Law. Once such a knowing is acquired, security lies in the stable, consistent, and collectively created field of Heart Wisdom.

Within the Grid, we have been trapped in our own collective agreements, leaving ourselves no space to experience anything other than suffering. Within this field, only insecurity can prevail. It is logical; it is the Law. The key to moving from a perennial state of insecurity

> *Sovereignty within cor publicum is a direct result of public engagement attuned with Heart Wisdom.*

to a field of security is courage. The key to freeing ourselves into *cor publicum* is courage.

Within the Grid, we have long defined courage as an egocentric and often self-serving act of martyrdom or heroism, thus unconsciously weakening our connection to security. As a result, we have gradually lost our courage. We have long been too afraid and contracted to find the courage to Love. It is the courage to Love, collectively, that creates the field of security. As long as we are embedded in the frame of reference of the mind, courage as it

> *The key to freeing ourselves into cor publicum is courage.*

pertains to Love is dismissed, refuted, ridiculed. It is when we find the courage to leap into the unknown, to leap into the never-experienced experience of collective Love, that security can be felt and found. And, any given specific collective form—such as a nation or a country—ultimately becomes irrelevant.

We have long been too afraid and contracted to find the courage to Love.

When the form itself is no longer equated with security, but security is generated from a collective that embraces and embodies *cor publicum,* the need for nations and countries and other rigidly structured forms of the Grid may become outdated.

Chapter 18

Educational Understandings in *Cor Publicum*

Education plays a pivotal role in society. Education reflects the underlying assumptions, values, and goals that society collectively holds and agrees to perpetuate. Education is the mirror of society, reflecting its light, reflecting its shadow, reflecting its jewels, reflecting its rotten fruits.

Within the framework of the Grid, education is primarily conceived as an accumulation of linear data compartmentalized in specialized areas, which a student learns to analyze, categorize, distribute, and consequentially organize. Nonlinear topics are approached merely through the discriminating lens of good and bad. As such, education is an expression of the lone monarch—the mind.

Within *cor publicum,* education is a lifelong journey of exploration. Education is conceived as a creative and innovative process to maximize the enjoyment of life guided by Heart Wisdom. Within *cor publicum,* self-reflection, self-responsibility, self-awareness, self-care, and most important, self-love and self-esteem, are core practices. Their power to instill respect, trust, hope, empathy, and compassion in the whole is recognized.

Education is the mirror of society, reflecting its light, reflecting its shadow, reflecting its jewels, reflecting its rotten fruits.

Within the Grid, joy and celebration are deemed to be forces distracting to the accumulation of wealth. In *cor publicum,* students learn the deeper meaning of joy and celebration and their impact on the wealth of society.

Within *cor publicum,* linear and nonlinear thinking are equally valued and fostered. Mental and emotional intelligence are equally emphasized and strengthened. Specialized and interdisciplinary approaches are held in equal esteem.

Within cor publicum, *education mirrors the multicolored facets of the whole, rather than a monochromatic section of the whole.*

Within the Grid, Heart Wisdom is marginal. Within *cor publicum,* Heart Wisdom is foundational.

Within *cor publicum,* education mirrors the multicolored facets of the whole, rather than a monochromatic section of the whole.

The teachings of the Heart are taught and practiced starting at an early age and recognized as essential to the functioning and thriving of society.

Remembering the innate ability to live in the Heart space is the starting point and the destination of education. The Heart space is the starting point for creative exploration of life in all its forms. The Heart space is the starting point for relating to life. The Heart space is the first and continuous breath offered to children and youth.

> *Remembering the innate ability to live in the Heart space is the starting point and the destination of education.*

Within *cor publicum,* the understandings of education are defined by each individual, each collective attuned to Heart Wisdom. The understandings of education are calibrated to the shades and colors of each individual and collective Heart. It is in the co-creative process, in the pulsating Heart, that the essential educational understandings emerge.

Chapter 19

Economic Understandings in *Cor Publicum*

Economics describes a value-driven exchange and is ultimately intended to maximize the well-being of society.

Economics within the Grid is a limited expression of the fundamental tendency of connection and co-creation to relax into abundance.

The economy within the Grid has become a contorted and twisted web of practices based on the old societal agreements: divide and conquer, denial, invariability, problem dependence, addiction to unhappiness, scarcity, and enslavement to time.

Economics within the Grid is the poor version of abundance.

Economics within the Grid is the caged version of free choice, the enslaved version of freedom, the inconsistent version of wealth.

Economics within the Grid is poverty disguised as abundance, control disguised as freedom and opportunity.

> *Economics within the Grid is the caged version of free choice, the enslaved version of freedom, the inconsistent version of wealth.*

Economics *per se* is a natural expression of human creativity and desire to share in the awareness of abundance. Within the cropped pyramidal structure of the Grid, economics has been a war against scarcity: this war is nothing more than the natural and logical consequence of the agreements held by a collective embedded in the Grid. Within the Grid, economics cannot be anything other than an expression of such agreements.

The debate over whether economics should be based on regulations or the so-called free market is irrelevant: it is an empty battle over nothingness, a battle between two illusionary opposites that are trapped in the same illusionary premise of scarcity.

> *Economics within the Grid is poverty disguised as abundance, control disguised as freedom and opportunity.*

The many economic theories are equally trapped in the tight confines of the mind, scrambling for a way out of scarcity, for the mirage of a long-lost abundance and wealth.

In a society where abundance and wealth are defined within the mind, not-enough-ness is perpetual, and wealth consistently decreases. In a society where abundance and wealth are experienced within the Heart, plenitude is reliable and consistently increases.

> *The debate over whether economics should be based on regulations or the so-called free market is irrelevant.*

The economy within the Grid is a dead-end road. The economy within *cor publicum* is a path leading to many sources.

Economics within the Grid focuses on how to reach an outcome. Economics within *cor publicum* relaxes into its natural outcome.

The economy of a society that assumes and experiences abundance beyond the narrowly defined terms of the mind is sustainable and flourishes. A society that is attuned to Heart Wisdom, to the needs of both the individual and the whole, calibrates its exchanges of resources

> *The economy within* cor publicum *is a path leading to many sources.*

with balance and engages in such exchanges with a conscious, broadened understanding of value.

A society that is attuned to Heart Wisdom allows the creative flow of the Heart Mind to maximize well-being, to maximize the enjoyment of resources. It is a society that exchanges creations, thus strengthening the overall matrix of the collective. Economics is not merely an exchange of goods and services, as practiced within the Grid. The physical and material expression of the vibrational web of society continuously informs the fundamental web of collective consciousness.

> *At the core of the economic exchange, there is a deeper exchange happening.*

At the core of the economic exchange, there is a deeper exchange happening between the economic web and the consciousness web of society. These webs simultaneously inform each other. Depending on the vibrational quality of the collective agreements, these webs either weaken or strengthen each other. The health of the "fundamental economy" (the consciousness web) determines the health and wealth of the "surface economy" (the economic web).

> *In the embracing of new collective agreements inspired and guided by Heart Wisdom, whole wealth is experienced.*

Within the Grid, the fundamental economy is deeply rooted in limitation and scarcity, thus creating unsustainable forms that continuously drain life force from the collective body. These limitations can generate only an unsustainable, ungrounded, and inflated version of wealth. The dearth of economic value of the collective agreements of the Grid has created a shaky and disintegrating surface economy.

Within *cor publicum,* the fundamental economy is deeply rooted in abundance, which continuously infuses life force into the collective body. This quality can generate only a sustainable, grounded version of wealth.

In the embracing of new collective agreements inspired and guided by Heart Wisdom, whole wealth is experienced. Well-being is lived.

Chapter 20

Health Understandings in *Cor Publicum*

Health is the premise of *cor publicum*. Disease is the premise of the Grid. In *cor publicum,* health is understood as a circular and interdependent web of cause and effect. Health is not compartmentalized in the realm of disease, but approached as a systemic web at different and intertwined levels of society.

> *Health is the premise of* cor publicum. *Disease is the premise of the Grid.*

Within *cor publicum,* health is balance within the individual body, and within the public body. The pervasive and increasing diseases within the Grid—even in areas of the world that are considered "wealthy"—are natural and simple consequences of the imbalance in the public body.

In *cor publicum,* the intimate, essential connection and interdependence of the individual body and the public body is understood and seen as the Heart-logical consequence of Law.

With this awareness, the health of the fundamental agreements and practices of the public body is scrutinized and continuously kept in balance with Heart Wisdom. It is recognized that the health of all relations is intimately reflected in the health of individual bodies.

In cor publicum, the intimate, essential connection and interdependence of the individual body and the public body is understood and seen as the Heart-logical consequence of Law.

From within the limited perspective of the Grid, the individual body is considered to be severed from the public body and even from itself. And, remedies to restore balance are sought from this cropped perspective.

When a disease is capable of being decoded from within the linear mind, a remedy is found. When a disease is uncontrollable from the standpoint of the mind, research scrambles to make sense of the complexity of life. Research is often inadequate, trying to catch a train that has long departed, and in the despair of its own impotence offers quick-fix remedies that—even when well meant— are often harmful to the individual and public bodies. Such remedies are harmful because they are disconnected from the reality of interconnectedness.

A society that embraces the agreements of *cor publicum* is one that embraces health. It is a society whose vibration beats continuously with each pulsation of the collective Heart, fostering and strengthening the health of the public body and thus of the individual body. It is a society that is capable of recognizing the Heart-logical connection between the practices of the collective and individual health. It is a society that carries responsibility for creating a healthy foundation for the individual to grow upon; a society where the individual embraces his own responsibility to infuse the collective with his own healthy practices.

> *A society operating from within the Grid is continuously at war with disease.*

A society operating from within the Grid is continuously at war with disease; it is a desperate society that does not know where to turn as it watches poisonous mushrooms pop up everywhere. It is a society powerless in the face of seemingly uncontrollable diseases, a society angry at its own frailty, a society that has lost its ability to understand and master the complexities of life, a society that is locked into the dead end of disintegration and debilitation, a society that screams at the public body to take care of the individual body, a society where individuals scream at their own bodies. It is a society that is losing its voice and whose body is rapidly disintegrating, because it is severed from the health that sustains life force. It is a society that in its desperation has created a self-poisoning disease machine.

Within *cor publicum,* individuals and collectives attuned to Heart Wisdom, attuned to responsibility, attuned to power, attuned to abundance, attuned to transparency, attuned to awareness, are freed from their self-created slavery and bring forth health with each Heart pulsation.

> *Within* cor publicum, *individuals and collectives strengthen with each pulsation the vibration of health.*

Within *cor publicum,* individuals and collectives strengthen with each pulsation the vibration of health; they infuse the collective body and thus the individual body with the frequency of balance; they are aware of and responsible for their own contributions to health; they gently support each other, where imbalance exists, to restore balance to the whole—within the individual body, and within the collective body.

Within *cor publicum,* individuals and collectives access the Heart Mind and allow Heart Wisdom to determine if, when, and how the formidable technologies developed by the Heart Mind are needed to restore balance. Individuals and collectives allow the Heart Mind to tap into the paradox and complexity of life to bring forth new life-sustaining forms to restore health; they bring about forms that are attuned to the health of both the collective and the individual bodies.

Cor publicum is a society that has chosen health and as a result embraces each individual and collective in this fundamental vibrational reality. Diseases are no longer at the core of the socioeconomic exchange of society; rather, they are a marginal situation in society.

> *A society that is immersed in its fear of the uncontrollable spreads with each pulsation a disease.*

In a society that generates a field of health with each pulsation, diseases are much less prone to spread or even develop. A society that is immersed in its fear of the uncontrollable spreads with each pulsation a disease. And, it continually creates new uncontrollable diseases as perfect mirrors of its own state of being.

A society that lives in Heart Wisdom and embraces the unknown factor is one that creates balance and health. It is a society that, rather than raising her fists at imbalance, wraps her arms around the imbalance. It is a society that in the calmness of wisdom is capable of accessing the complex web of life and of realigning the individual and collective with balance.

> *A society that lives in Heart Wisdom and embraces the unknown factor is one that creates balance and health.*

Chapter 21

Environmental Understandings in *Cor Publicum*

Within the Grid, the environmental condition of our planet is approached either as a battle of ideas, a battle of truths, a war over seemingly conflicting data, a race against time, or as a non-issue. The environment is perceived either as an overwhelming reminder of powerlessness or a mere marginal aspect of our existence. Overall, the environment is embedded in a polluted vibrational field of the warring mind.

> *Within the Grid, the environment is perceived either as an overwhelming reminder of powerlessness or a mere marginal aspect of our existence.*

Within *cor publicum,* the environmental situation is accepted, the environment embraced by Heart Wisdom, and the co-creative process activated. The environment is approached in its own right. Overall, the environment is embraced in a vibrational field of Love.

Within *cor publicum,* there is awareness and mastery of Law. Thus, the individual and the collective do not perceive themselves and act based on the assumption that they are separate from the environment. There is awareness that a collective attuned to Heart Wisdom infuses the environmental field with health and life force.

Cor publicum is a sustainable human matrix living in balance with all relationships, including our relationship with the land. Collective power is accessed to the benefit of all, including the environment. Collective power accesses land power, and both consciousnesses interplay and exchange to adjust to each other's needs, to the ever-changing environment, to the ever-changing humanity.

Within the Grid, the collective is engaged in a senseless battle, arguing over whether environmental changes are happening and who is to blame for the changes. Within *cor publicum,* change Is, and it is integrated and included in the continuous process of creating sustainable forms. The collective brings about change while surrendering to change.

Within *cor publicum,* the environment is consciously and thus effectively linked to the web of the collective, and the collective is consciously linked to the environment. Both respond to each other's changes; both sustain each other's life force—as the basic premise of engagement.

Within the Grid, the environment and the collective perceive each other as separate, two deaf and deadening entities screaming at each other, both changing, both unresponsive, and both rapidly disintegrating into formlessness.

Within cor publicum, *the environment is consciously and thus effectively linked to the web of the collective, and the collective is consciously linked to the environment.*

Within the Grid, change is curbed, resisted, and feared. Within *cor publicum,* change is an opportunity to choose again.

Within the Grid, time is either running out, or it is a given. Within *cor publicum,* power is accessed and the choice of time made.

Within the Grid, change happens only in linear time. Within *cor publicum,* change happens in the band of time beyond time; change is freed from the linear constraint and becomes exponential.

Within the Grid, the environment is struggling. Within *cor publicum,* the environment is detoxifying and seeking to conceive itself again on a healthy societal foundation.

Chapter 22

The Language of
Cor Publicum

The source of words can be recognized with ease. The language of the mind is often contorted, complicated, leading the reader into the maze of the mind with no easy way out. The language of the Heart is simple, short, essential.

Laws (lowercase), regulations, statutes, "legitimate" official and unofficial documents, and academic writings relating to the many systems of the Grid are articulated in the convulsed, adversarial, and impenetrable language of the mind. This language is meant to preserve separation and misunderstanding, meant to feed the battle of ideas and perpetuate confusion and powerlessness.

> *The language of* cor publicum *is sharp in its clarity, vertical in its direction, aiming like an arrow along the vector of collective intention.*

Law, directions, and guidance emerging from the systems of *cor publicum* are articulated in accessible, concise, clear, and transparent language. The language of *cor publicum* is also sensorial, imaginative, musical. It is a language that is freed from the linear constraint of words. It is a universal language that lifts the barrier created by words; it is a pervasive language that taps into the language beyond words. It is the language of the Heart, which strengthens communication, strengthens the matrix of society, strengthens the quality of the social contract, and strengthens the pulsation and life force of a grounded, compact, and vibrant collective body.

> *The language of* cor publicum *is self-evident. The language within the Grid scrambles for evidence.*

The language of *cor publicum* is sharp in its clarity, vertical in its direction, aiming like an arrow along the vector of collective intention. The language within the Grid is muddled, aimless, pointing in many directions, and leading into multiple tangents, slowing and at times blocking the emergence of a vector of intention, and causing collective intention to drown in a sea of confusing words.

Language in *cor publicum* serves its citizens. Language within the Grid is self-serving.

Language in *cor publicum* is a path. Language within the Grid is a roadblock.

Language in *cor publicum* is grounded in its simplicity. Language within the Grid is scattered in the mental ether.

In *cor publicum,* language is a means of fostering communication. Within the Grid, language is a means of obstructing communication.

The language of *cor publicum* welcomes stillness. The language of the Grid stimulates restlessness.

The language of *cor publicum* is self-evident. The language within the Grid scrambles for evidence.

The language of *cor publicum* is layered in its impact and consistent with its intention. The language within the Grid is layered in its intentions and consistent with its impact.

The language of *cor publicum* cherishes essence. The language within the Grid is ignorant of essence.

The language of the mind challenges life. The language of the Heart sustains life.

Chapter 23

Re-Founding
into *Cor Publicum*

The re-founding into *cor publicum* is a gradual process or a sudden leap, depending on the vibrational environment of a given collective.

In the beginning, the re-founding is a gradual process, as individuals and collectives ponder the possibility of a fundamentally new social contract and its implications on governance. Thereafter, when the vector of intention is established by a few collectives, others follow. Once 2.5% of worldwide collectives align with *cor publicum,* many more collectives join in a sudden leap, facilitated by the increased collective Heart vibration.

> *The re-founding into* cor publicum *is a gradual process or a sudden leap.*

> *The re-founding is not a formal process within the systems of the Grid.*

The re-founding is not a formal process within the systems of the Grid. Any engagement with and within the systems of the Grid is *per se* incapable of conceiving and generating anything other than forms of Grid consciousness.

The re-founding is an organic process, an act of choice, individually and collectively, a practice, an embodiment. It is a creative process that generates new systems, a creative process that Is new governance.

> *The re-founding is an organic process, an act of choice, individually and collectively, a practice, an embodiment.*

As long as the collective limits its range of choices to the systems of the Grid, it will perennially find itself living in, coping with, or fighting against the systems it has unconsciously generated.

The creation of a new social contract is a sovereign act that flows from the power of each individual. It is not an act that requires "permission" from an illusionary outside "entity." *Cor publicum* is not the result of a formal process. *Cor publicum* is activated by the sovereign act of choice.

> Cor publicum *is not a result. It is the beginning.*

Cor publicum is not a result. It is the beginning.

There are no hurdles, no limitations, no deadlines, no prerequisites. *Cor publicum* is the act of choice of an individual and a collective to live in alignment with Heart Wisdom within the collective body; it is the choice to embody Heart Wisdom; it is the choice to consciously connect with each other as collective bodies; it is the choice to co-create in the awareness of the responsibility, freedom, and power that each being already holds.

> *The re-founding of* cor publicum *can happen in a heartbeat.*

The re-founding of *cor publicum* is cracking the illusion that power has to be given to individuals and collectives before they can determine their form of governance. Within the Grid, this illusion has generated a lifeless, waiting, and complaining collective. The re-founding of *cor publicum* can happen in a heartbeat: no waiting, no complaining, no sleepless sleep. The opportunity of a new choice is ever-present, inherent in the Law governing existence, and sustained by Heart Wisdom.

It is through the embodiment of collective Heart Power by individuals, and the embodiment of individual Heart Power by collectives, that *cor publicum* is activated and the creative process is set into motion. It is through movement along the vector of collective Heart intention that *many* forms of governance attuned to each collective emerge.

In this regard, *cor publicum* is governance of governance. It is the vibrational life-sustaining blueprint of governance out of which various forms of governance emerge. *Cor publicum* holds the vibrational qualities of freedom, power, responsibility, equality, and abundance, and the vibrational capacity to access them. *Cor publicum* holds Law. *Cor publicum* offers the key to access the fundamental pillar of governance: Heart Wisdom.

> *Cor publicum*
> *is governance of*
> *governance. It is*
> *the vibrational life-*
> *sustaining blueprint*
> *of governance out*
> *of which various*
> *forms of governance*
> *emerge.*

The re-founding into *cor publicum* begins with a journey into our Hearts, an often dreaded, painful, avoided, unfamiliar, and uncomfortable exploration. It is an obligatory passage that collectively we have refused to take, which has resulted in much suffering and confusion. The courage to walk this mysterious and (to the mind) senseless and terrifying path, lands us into our collective Heart. Here resides what we have been chasing for eons: freedom, power, equality, abundance, and responsibility—the fundamental pillars of how we want to live individually and with each other.

The re-founding of *cor publicum* continues with a transparent and open collective conversation about the Grid, and about the elements of *cor publicum*.

The re-founding continues with a statement of collective intention and attunement to Heart Wisdom.

It continues with the co-creative process revealing the many forms—the how—the life force of *cor publicum*.

It continues when we link the many forms of *cor publicum* to each other.

It continues to expand and pulsate, sustaining a vibrant worldwide web, linked by the technology of the Heart and capable of turning the seemingly insurmountable problems affecting humanity into a field of opportunity.

It continues with a collective transformed by the life-sustaining forms flowing from the Heart Mind.

It continues with a collective capable of embracing itself with gentle, caring, and nurturing arms.

It continues with a collective capable of relaxing into itself.

It continues with a collective that relearns to play.

And it continues....

Chapter 24

Web of *Cor Publici*

A new emerging international form may be a web of *cor publici*. The *modus operandi* of *cor publicum* is applicable at any scale and fractal in nature.

Within *cor publicum,* the awareness is held that any local situation has a planetary implication, and every planetary situation has a local implication.

Within the Grid, this interdependence is addressed as a conflict—a conflict of interests, a conflict of data, a conflict of jurisdiction. Within *cor publicum,* this interdependence is integrated and held in the framing of the co-creative process, and accessed through Heart Wisdom in the collective, local, and planetary Heart. The local or planetary aspects of a situation are drawn into the co-creative process as essential complementary, non-conflicting ingredients in the quest for balance.

> *The* modus operandi *of* cor publicum *is applicable at any scale.*

As 2.5% of humanity organizes itself as a web of *cor publici,* the perceived conflict of interdependence loses its life force. And, the web creates a strong field of co-creative engagement, capable of effectively approaching what is occurring on a planetary level.

> *As 2.5% of humanity organizes itself as a web* of cor publici, *the conflict of interdependence loses its life force.*

This is the end of politics, the end of war, and the beginning of peace.

Epilogue

Recognizing
Cor Publicum

Cor publicum is recognized in the silence of the Heart.

Forms generating from within the Grid claim to reflect Heart Wisdom, and market themselves as such.

Forms generating from *cor publicum* are Heart Wisdom, silently and through their actions.

Within the Grid, concepts are generated, and freedom, power, peace, security, democracy, love, wealth, and integrity are claimed.

Within *cor publicum,* practices are embodied, and freedom, power, Love, safety, abundance, and integrity are experienced.

About the Author

Photograph by Lisi Wolf

Dr. Franca Baroni holds a J.D. equivalent and a doctorate in law from the University of Basle, Switzerland, and a master's in comparative law (L.L.M.) from the University of Miami. She is a member of the New York Bar since 1999 and a member of the Swiss Bar since 1997. She is a certified mediator with the Supreme Court of Florida and a meditation and awareness guide, not aligned with any particular tradition. She lives in Seattle, Washington.